Si: To Jane, my wife, and my three boys for their constant support and patience with my absences from home. Couldn't have done it all without you.

LA
E
2(

NEW YORK 3147

ISLES OF SCILLY 28
LONGSHIPS LIGHTHOUSE 1½

JOHN O'GROATS 874

HAIRY BIKERS
FOOD ♥ TOUR

Dave: To my family – Lili, the most patient and gorgeous woman in the world, Iza and Sergiu, for keeping me on my toes and making me happy.

WEIDENFELD & NICOLSON

Amanda Ross, Executive Producer of the Hairy Bikers Food Tour of Britain, would like to thank everyone involved at Cactus TV and the BBC in making the programme and Orion for a great book.

Compiled and edited for Cactus TV by Amanda Ross and Anna Ratcliffe
Graphics by Will Learmonth and Mike Afford
Photography by Rory McKellar, Cristian Barnett, Mark Law and Jonathan Farber
(page 53 ©Jonathan Farber Photography)

First published in hardback in Great Britain in 2009
by Orion Books an imprint of the Orion Publishing Group Ltd
Orion House, 5 Upper St Martin's Lane, London WC2H 9EA
an Hachette Livre UK Company

1 3 5 7 9 10 8 6 4 2

A CIP catalogue record for this book is available from the British Library.

ISBN: 978 0 29785 974 1

Design Kate Barr
Edited by Jinny Johnson
Proofread by Elise See Tai
Index by Elizabeth Wiggans

Printed in Spain by Cayfosa

The Orion Publishing Group's policy is to use papers that are natural, renewable and recyclable and made from wood grown in sustainable forests. The logging and manufacturing processes are expected to conform to the environmental regulations of the country of origin.

Every effort has been made to fulfil requirements with regard to reproducing copyright material. The author and publisher will be glad to rectify any omissions at the earliest opportunity.

www.orionbooks.co.uk

Back in the saddle

During the winter of 2008–2009 we made an epic journey round the UK.
We travelled 15,000 miles, through what happened to be the worst weather for
years, and visited 30 counties. And let us make one thing clear from the start –
there were no trailers or cars involved in the making of this project. It was us. On
our bikes. In the snow and rain.

We discovered that Britain has gone food mad. Everywhere we went we found
dedicated, passionate food producers and chefs. It is thanks to their generosity and
knowledge that we have been able to write this book, which is a fantastic shop
window for the food of this country. (In the back you will find a list of the suppliers
we visited so you can try them for yourself.)

In every county we met some of the best and most interesting farmers, growers
and suppliers – people producing beef and cheese and other favourites, as well
as lesser-known treasures such as dulse and cassis. Having found out about the
food of the region, we cooked a traditional recipe in our mobile kitchen – always
great fun. This was often a local dish that has been loved for centuries but was
perhaps in danger of becoming slightly forgotten. We found that people's interest
was quickly aroused and we were usually inundated with ideas and opinions.

We also visited a top chef in each county and they generously shared their secrets
and tips with us. Then we put our necks on the line and had a cook-off with each
of these chefs, both of us making dishes to showcase the local produce. These
were presented to a panel of local foodies. They didn't know who had cooked
what and had to judge which plate best represented the county. Sometimes we
won, sometimes the chef did, but whatever the outcome we ended up with some
great recipes.

Many of these dishes are made up of a number of parts. You might prefer to make
just one or two of these, or combine one part of one recipe with something in
another. Don't be a slave to convention – just dip in and mix and match as you like,
and you'll find some great ideas.

We were astonished at how strongly individual our counties are and how much the
food reflects the landscape and personality of a region. At the end of it all we came
to the conclusion that we have the best food and the best chefs in the world. So
join us in our celebration of the Best of Britain.

County chef:
David Littlewood
Restaurant:
The Milton

The Milton is set on the banks of the beautiful River Dee and is one of the area's leading restaurants. David is only 26 but is already a rising star in the food world. He has won a number of awards, such as Grampian Chef of the Year in 2007, and was a finalist in the Scottish Chef of the Year competition in 2009. He and his team turn out stunning dishes, some of which take a fresh look at Scottish classics, and the food looks as good as it tastes. David loves to cook with local produce and sources most of his ingredients within eight miles of the restaurant. He lists all his suppliers on the restaurant website.

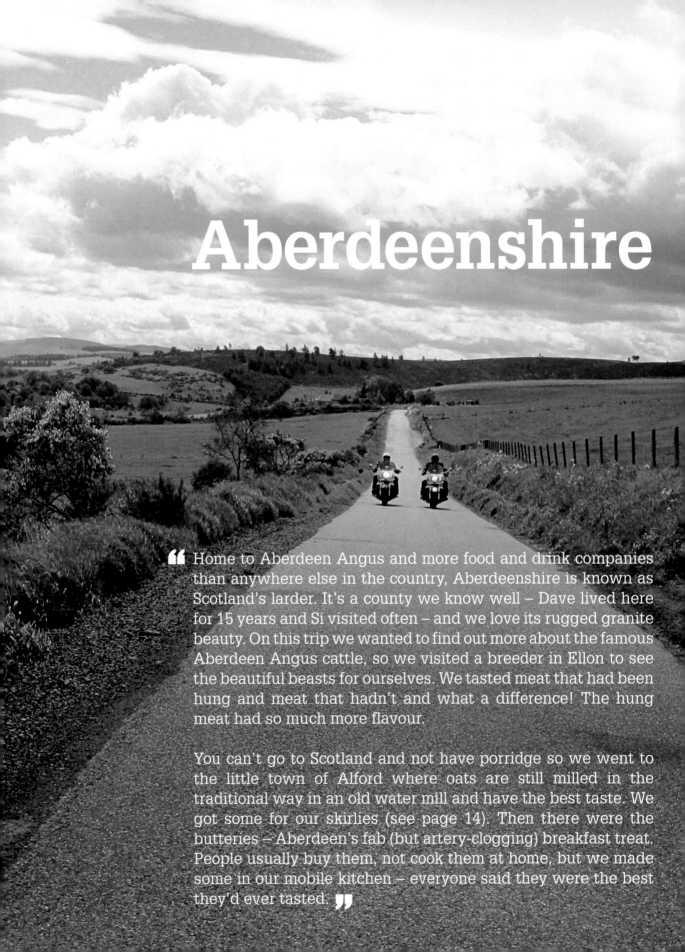

Aberdeenshire

"Home to Aberdeen Angus and more food and drink companies than anywhere else in the country, Aberdeenshire is known as Scotland's larder. It's a county we know well – Dave lived here for 15 years and Si visited often – and we love its rugged granite beauty. On this trip we wanted to find out more about the famous Aberdeen Angus cattle, so we visited a breeder in Ellon to see the beautiful beasts for ourselves. We tasted meat that had been hung and meat that hadn't and what a difference! The hung meat had so much more flavour.

You can't go to Scotland and not have porridge so we went to the little town of Alford where oats are still milled in the traditional way in an old water mill and have the best taste. We got some for our skirlies (see page 14). Then there were the butteries – Aberdeen's fab (but artery-clogging) breakfast treat. People usually buy them, not cook them at home, but we made some in our mobile kitchen – everyone said they were the best they'd ever tasted. "

Aberdeen Butteries (Rowies)

These are a traditional breakfast treat in Aberdeenshire. True to their name, there's an awful lot of butter in them, as well as a bit of lard – perhaps that's why they taste so very scrumptious!

Makes 16

500g strong plain flour, plus extra for rolling
1 sachet easy-blend dried yeast
1 tbsp soft light-brown sugar
1 tbsp flaked sea salt
350ml warm water
275g butter
100g lard
oil, for greasing

Mix the flour, yeast, sugar and salt together in a large bowl. Make a well in the centre and pour in the water. Stir with a wooden spoon and then mix with your hands to form a ball. Turn out on to a floured surface and knead for 10 minutes until the dough is smooth and pliable. Put in a clean bowl, cover with a piece of oiled clingfilm and leave to rise in a warm place for about an hour, or until doubled in size.

Cream the butter and lard together and divide into 4 portions. Turn the dough on to a floured surface and knead for a minute. Using a rolling pin, roll into a rectangle roughly 40cm x 20cm and about 1cm thick. Spread 1 portion of the butter mixture over the bottom two-thirds of the rectangle. Fold the remaining third of the dough over on to the butter mixture, then lift the bottom third over that to give 2 layers of fat between the dough. Make a quarter turn, then roll the dough back to its original size. Repeat the fat spreading, folding and rolling stages 3 times more, until all the butter and lard mixture is used up.

tip:
Cheesy butteries are delicious, too – just add some grated cheese to the dough. Great spread with a little marmite.

Preheat the oven to 200°C/Gas 6. Cut the dough into 16 pieces and shape each one into a round flat bun shape. Place the buns on to lightly oiled baking trays and leave to rise for a further 45 minutes or until light and puffy. Bake for about 18 minutes or until slightly risen and golden brown. Cool on wire racks or serve warm. Spread each buttery thickly with yet more butter and top with marmalade or jam.

David Littlewood's Roe Deer

with potato dumplings, kale, parsnip purée and pearl barley sauce

In this recipe, the venison is prepared in two different ways to suit the different characteristics of the meat – the shin is slow cooked and the rack is roasted. Roe deer is best for both if possible. Ask your butcher to French trim the rack of venison and remove the chain bone. And if you can't get the black kale, use savoy cabbage.

Serves 4

Venison and sauce
1 rack of venison (8 ribs)
50g unsalted butter
3 sprigs of fresh thyme
6 shallots
1 large carrot
3 celery sticks
1 garlic bulb, cut in half
4 pieces of venison shin
vegetable oil
30g tomato purée
200ml red wine (Cabernet Sauvignon)
1 litre venison stock
50g pearl barley (soaked in cold water)

Dumplings
1kg starchy potatoes
100g butter
150g flour

4 eggs
100g baby spinach,
    washed and shredded
grated nutmeg to taste
oil for frying

Creamed black kale
4 shallots, finely chopped
1 garlic clove
80g Alford pancetta, diced
20g butter
400g black kale, washed and shredded
100ml cream

Parsnip purée
4 parsnips, peeled and roughly
    chopped
1 litre milk
55g butter

To roast the venison ribs
Preheat the oven to 190°C/Gas 5. Season the rack well and seal it in a hot pan, then add a knob of the butter and a sprig of thyme. Remove the pan from the heat and don't allow the butter to burn. Spoon the butter over the meat and transfer it to a roasting tin. Pour any butter left in the pan over the meat and roast for about 8 minutes for medium-rare meat. Leave the meat to rest.

To slow-cook the venison shin

Preheat the oven to 180°C/Gas 4. Peel and chop the vegetables into 3cm dice. Season the meat well with salt and pepper and colour in vegetable oil in a very hot pan until dark brown on all sides. Transfer to a casserole dish. Deglaze the browning pan with a little water and add this to the meat.

Melt the rest of the butter in the pan and cook the vegetables in the butter until golden brown, add the tomato purée and cook for a further minute. Add this to the meat. Pour the red wine into the casserole and reduce until it becomes a glaze. Add the rest of the thyme and the garlic and venison stock to the casserole and bring it to the boil.

Cover with greaseproof paper and cook in the oven for 1½–2 hours, or until tender. Remove the meat and keep warm. Pass the stock through a sieve, then pour it back into a saucepan, reduce by half and season. Set aside for the sauce.

To make the sauce

Drain the pearl barley, place it in a small saucepan and cover with cold water. Bring to the boil, then reduce the heat and simmer until tender. Strain and add to the reduced stock from the venison shin to create the sauce.

To make the dumplings

Wash the potatoes and cook them in slightly salted water until soft (about 20 minutes). Leave to cool slightly, then peel and mash them, as if making mashed potatoes. Return the potatoes to a very low heat, stirring with a wooden spoon until they no longer stick to the sides of the pot.

While the potatoes are boiling, make the dough. Boil 225ml of water with the butter and a pinch of salt. Remove from the heat and add the flour all at once, mixing vigorously until absorbed, then put the mixture back on a low heat to dry out slightly.

Remove the mixture from the heat and add the eggs, one at a time, and mix until you have a dough that is still wet and slightly sticky. Mix the potatoes and the dough together in the ratio of one-third potato to two-thirds dough. Add the spinach and nutmeg and season with salt and pepper to taste.

Heat several inches of oil in a pan or deep-fat fryer to 180°C and carefully drop a tablespoon (or quenelle if you want to show off!) of the mixture into the oil. Allow the mixture to puff up and brown before removing it to drain on paper towels. Repeat for the required number of servings. Any unused mixture will keep, covered, for a couple of days in the fridge.

To prepare the creamed kale

Sweat the shallots, garlic and pancetta in a hot pan with the butter, add the kale and cook for 2–3 minutes. Add the cream and reduce for 1–2 minutes, then season.

To prepare the parsnip purée

Put the parsnips in a large pan and cover with milk. Place on a high heat until the milk just starts to steam, reduce the heat and cook until the parsnips are tender. Strain, then pile into a food processor with the butter and process until smooth. Season with salt and pepper.

to serve:

Carve the venison rack between every second rib bone. On each plate, place a spoonful of kale and sit a piece of shin on top. Spoon or pipe a little parsnip purée next to this. Place the venison rack and potato dumplings on the other side of the shin and drizzle with the barley sauce.

Aberdeen Angus Beef Olives

with kidney gravy, skirlies and champit potatoes

Skirlies are traditionally a stuffing, but can also be served on the side. Medium oatmeal can be used for skirlies, but some people prefer to use half pinhead and half coarse oatmeal to give a rougher texture. Champit potatoes are a bit like Irish Champ – ours is a luxury version. Swede, a traditional Scottish vegetable, and some puréed carrots make good accompaniments to this.

Serves 4

Beef olives

4 featherblade or sirloin steaks
   or slices of topside
4 rashers streaky bacon, finely chopped
1 onion, finely chopped
75g fresh breadcrumbs
75g shredded beef suet
½ tsp dried mixed herbs
2 tsp finely chopped parsley
zest of ½ lemon
1 tsp lemon juice
100g good pork sausage meat
½ tsp sea salt flakes
½ tsp ground black pepper
1 egg, beaten
1 tbsp Scottish mustard
2 tbsp seasoned flour
2 tbsp olive oil
knob of butter
2 onions, finely sliced
175g kidneys, cored and diced

1 tbsp flour
100ml red wine
300ml good beef stock
1 tbsp tomato purée

Skirlies

50g shredded beef suet
1 onion, finely chopped
175g oatmeal
2–3 tbsp good chicken stock
1 tbsp rapeseed oil, for frying

Champit potatoes

1kg good floury potatoes, peeled
   and cut into even-sized pieces
100ml full-fat milk
2 tbsp sour cream
4 spring onions, very finely chopped
50g butter
2 tsp chopped chives

To prepare the beef olives and kidney gravy

Preheat the oven to 170°C/Gas 3. Place a piece of clingfilm over the steaks and beat them out until they are really thin. To make the stuffing, mix together the chopped bacon and onion, breadcrumbs, suet, mixed herbs, parsley, lemon zest and juice, sausage meat, sea salt and black pepper, and add the beaten egg.

Lay the beef slices out flat and spread with a thin layer of mustard. Divide the stuffing between the steaks, spreading it on top of the mustard. Roll each piece of meat up into a tube shape and secure with butcher's string. Dust the beef olives with seasoned flour.

Heat the olive oil and the butter in a casserole dish and shallow fry the beef olives until brown all over. Take them out and set aside, keeping the fat and beef juices in the dish. Add the sliced onions and cook until translucent. Add the kidneys and brown, then add a tablespoon of flour and cook gently for 1–2 minutes. Pour in the wine, stock and tomato purée and bring to a simmer.

Put the beef olives back in the casserole and spoon over the juices. Place in the oven for about 1 hour, until the meat is cooked and the sauce is nice and thick. The gravy can be strained and reduced if you prefer, but we like a few bits of onion and kidney in ours.

To make the skirlies

Melt the suet in a heavy frying pan. Add the onion and cook slowly until translucent. Add the oatmeal and fry for 5 minutes until nicely toasted. Pour in the chicken stock and cook, stirring constantly, until the oats soften and the mixture comes together. Press into a chef's ring, then turn them out to make 4 skirlies. Heat the oil in a frying pan and fry the skirlies for 2–3 minutes on each side until golden.

To make the champit potatoes

Boil the potatoes until soft in plenty of salted water. Pass them through a sieve or a potato ricer into a bowl and keep warm. Gently heat the milk and sour cream in a pan, then add the spring onions and cook for a couple of minutes to soften them, stirring regularly. Don't overheat or the sour cream will curdle. Stir the mixture into the mashed potatoes, then add the butter and chives and season to taste.

to serve:
Slice the beef olives and place some on each plate with a skirlie alongside. Add the champit – and the swede and the carrot purée if serving – and spoon over the gravy.

County chef:
Stephen Duffy
Restaurant:
Noelle's

Chef Stephen Duffy lives
in Anglesey and has been
cooking in Wales for the past
18 years. He's won both the
North Wales Chef of the Year
and Young Welsh Chef of the
Year awards and belongs to
the UK's Craft Guild of Chefs.
Noelle's is the restaurant at
Tre-Ysgawen Hall, one of the
leading country house hotels
in Wales. Stephen is a firm
supporter of local produce
and believes that Welsh black
beef and hand-dived Anglesey
scallops are the best in the
world. He grows herbs and
many of the vegetables for
the kitchen in the hotel's
walled garden and is proud
to get 98 per cent of his
produce from Anglesey.

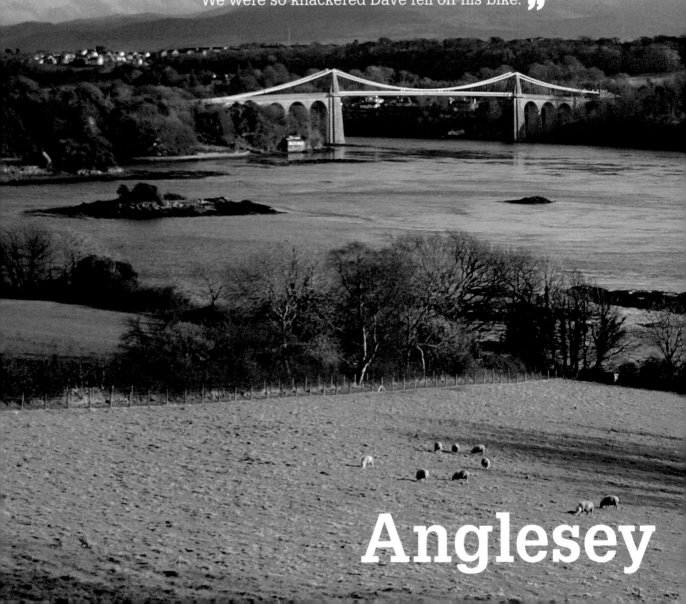

> " We didn't know what to expect from Anglesey and we were amazed. It's stunningly beautiful, we got a great welcome and the food was phenomenal. We learned about Halen Mon sea salt, which comes from here and is the very best – used by many top chefs – and we visited the wonderful Hooton's farm where we picked Welsh leeks and collected eggs for our Anglesey egg dish. We also went gathering some of Anglesey's superb mussels. Did you know that 50 per cent of the mussels sold in Europe come from the Menai Strait? And that those grown on mud beds have more flavour? Anyway, there we were, lying on our bellies in the mud, scraping mussels into a basket while a howling wind whistled about our ears. Then we had to drag the laden baskets back to the beach. It was the hardest day ever – we'll appreciate mussels all the more now. We were so knackered Dave fell off his bike. "

Anglesey

Anglesey Eggs

This is a great way to use up any left-over potatoes and hard bits of cheese you have lying around in the fridge, and it's even more delicious when served with a smoked bacon chop.

Serves 4

500g potatoes, peeled and chopped
knob of butter
salt and ground white pepper
80–110ml double cream
3 leeks, sliced
8 eggs
extra butter for greasing dish

Sauce
50g unsalted butter
50g plain flour
600ml milk
1 tsp mustard powder
75g Cheddar cheese, grated
75g Caerphilly cheese, grated

Topping
100g white breadcrumbs
25g Cheddar cheese, grated
25g Caerphilly cheese, grated
pinch of ground nutmeg
salt and pepper

To serve
olive oil
8 smoked bacon chops
1 small handful of flat-leaf parsley,
    chopped

Cook the potatoes in boiling, salted water, then drain and pass them through a potato ricer into a clean pan. Add the butter, white pepper, salt and cream and mix over a gentle heat. Cook the leeks in a pan of boiling water for 3–4 minutes, then drain. Stir the cooked leeks into the mash.

tip:
When making mash, it's good to poach the potatoes in simmering water, rather than boil them. It improves the texture. Also, after draining the potatoes, put them back on the heat to dry out for a few minutes.

Mix together all the topping ingredients in a large bowl and set aside. For the sauce, melt the butter in a pan, then add the flour and cook over a low heat for 1–2 minutes. Pour in the milk and whisk over a moderate heat until the mixture thickens. Add the mustard powder and seasoning, then stir in the combined cheeses until melted.

Preheat the oven to 200°C/Gas 6. Boil the eggs for 8–10 minutes, then drain and cool under running water. Peel the eggs and slice them into rings. Grease an ovenproof dish with butter. Spoon the mash into the dish and press it down. Arrange the egg slices on top of the mash, overlapping them in a circular pattern if you like. Season with salt and pepper and then pour over the cheese sauce.

to serve:
Spoon the Anglesey eggs on to serving plates and serve the crispy bacon chops alongside. Garnish with flat-leaf parsley to finish.

Sprinkle on the crumb topping, then place the dish on a baking tray. Bake in the oven for 20–25 minutes or until golden brown and bubbling. Meanwhile, heat a little olive oil in a non-stick frying pan and pan-fry the bacon chops on each side for 3–4 minutes, or until crisp and cooked through.

Stephen Duffy's Fillet of Welsh Black Beef

with creamed swede, horseradish mashed potatoes and gratin of wild smoked mushrooms

We tasted some great beef while making the series – beef from Scotland, Wales and England – but this Welsh black beef was certainly one of the best. This recipe shows it off well.

Serves 4

Beef and vegetables
1 small swede
250g unsalted butter
250g Anglesey potatoes
125ml double cream
20g horseradish sauce
500g smoked shiitake mushrooms
4 x 225g fillets of beef
butter
olive oil

Basil jelly
250g fresh basil
5g agar agar

Shallot purée
300g shallots
olive oil

Sabayon
125g butter
250g dried mixed mushrooms
4 egg yolks

Sauce
75ml port
3 sprigs of thyme

To prepare the basil jelly
Blanch the basil in a pan of boiling water for 30 seconds. Drain, put the basil into a blender and blitz to a fine consistency. Pass the basil through a fine sieve with a bowl underneath to collect the basil juice. Add the agar agar to the basil juice and pour into a rectangular dish lined with clingfilm. Leave to cool and set in the fridge. Once set, cut the jelly into small 1cm cubes and keep in the fridge until ready to serve.

To make the shallot purée
Preheat the oven to 140°C/Gas 1. Place the shallots in a roasting tray with some olive oil and season with salt and pepper. Roast for 40 minutes until soft. Set 2 whole shallots aside and place the rest in a blender. Blitz to a fine purée and then pass through a sieve.

To make the sabayon

Melt the butter in a pan. Put the dried mushrooms into a coffee grinder or blender and reduce to a very fine powder. Whisk the egg yolks in a large metal or glass bowl. Add the mushroom powder to the egg yolks and mix well. Place the bowl over a saucepan of boiling water and gradually add the butter, whisking constantly. Return to a gentle heat and continue to whisk until there are 'ribbon trails' in the sabayon and you can see the path of the whisk in the bottom of the bowl. Keep warm so the sabayon doesn't split before serving.

To prepare the beef and vegetables

Peel and chop the swede and cook it in boiling water until soft. Drain and purée the swede in a blender. Stir in 110g of the butter, season and then pass the purée through a sieve to remove any lumps. Keep it warm until ready to serve.

Next, peel, wash and chop the potatoes and cook in boiling, salted water until soft. Pass them through a potato ricer for silky smooth mash or just mash them well, making sure there are no lumps. Add the rest of the butter and the cream and horseradish, then season and set aside. Heat a pan with butter and sweat the smoked shiitake mushrooms until cooked, then set aside. Season the steaks. Heat some butter and oil in a large frying pan, then seal the steaks on both sides. Cook for 8–10 minutes for rare meat and leave to rest.

To make the sauce

Pour the port into a pan and add the cooking juices from the fillet steaks. Add the thyme and reduce over a low heat until the sauce is about half its original volume.

to serve:

In 4 small presentation copper pans or similar, arrange the smoked shiitake mushrooms in the bottom and spoon the sabayon on top. Take the 2 whole shallots from the roasting tin and cut in half length-ways. Place a half on top of the sabayon in each pan and glaze under a hot grill for a few minutes. Warm the plates. Spoon and drag a quenelle of swede to one side and pipe some mash on the other. Pour on some sauce and add a steak. Then add a few cubes of the basil jelly and some shallot purée.

Seafood
with a true flavour of Anglesey

This dish uses three great Anglesey ingredients – mussels, oysters and sea salt. The shellfish are world famous and the salt is second to none. Don't feel you have to make everything at once. The mussels and chips would make a lovely supper and you could try the oysters and other things another night.

Serves 4–6

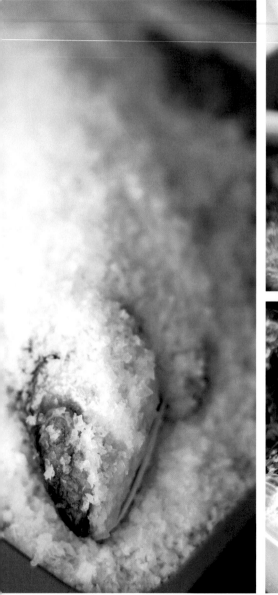

Sea bass

2 sea bass, scaled and gutted

2 garlic cloves, peeled

1 lemon, cut into slices

2kg rock salt

pinch of pure sea salt with vanilla

Cabbage

50g butter

1 spring cabbage, finely shredded

1 leek, finely shredded

125ml fish stock

110ml double cream

salt and pepper

Corn-crusted oysters

vegetable oil, for deep-frying

12 oysters

1 cup of cornmeal

1 tbsp ground cumin

1 tsp ground fennel

pinch of Anglesey spiced sea salt

2 eggs

splash of milk

Chips

vegetable oil for deep-frying

4 potatoes, peeled

wedge of lemon

sea salt diamonds

Mussels with leeks

1 leek, sliced

2 celery sticks, sliced

2 shallots, chopped

50g butter

2 bay leaves

1 small bunch of thyme

½ bottle white wine

2kg mussels, cleaned and de-bearded

1 handful of flat-leaf parsley, chopped

pinch of Anglesey celery salt

To prepare the fish

Preheat the oven to 180°C/Gas 4. Wash the sea bass and pat them dry, then put a lightly bashed clove of garlic and a few slices of lemon in the gut cavity of each fish. Line a roasting tin with a bed of rock salt – the cheap stuff is fine for this – and place the fish on top. Cover the fish with the remaining rock salt, sprinkle with water and press the salt down to cover the fish. Bake in the oven for 25–30 minutes.

When the fish is cooked and has cooled slightly, begin to remove the salt by gently breaking some off. Brush the rest of the rock salt off the skin with a pastry brush and remove the flesh from the fish.

To cook the cabbage

Melt the butter in a large pan and sauté the cabbage and leek for a few minutes to soften. Add the fish stock and cream and continue to cook for 5–6 minutes until the liquid has reduced but is still creamy. Season to taste.

To prepare the oysters

Heat the vegetable oil in a pan ready for deep frying. Meanwhile, using an oyster knife, carefully open the oysters, remove them from the shell and set aside to drain on kitchen paper. Mix the cornmeal, ground cumin, ground fennel and spiced sea salt in a bowl.

In a separate bowl, whisk the eggs with a splash of milk. Dip the oysters into the egg mixture, then into the spiced cornmeal. Deep-fry the oysters in the hot oil for 1 minute or until golden brown. Remove with a slotted spoon and drain on kitchen paper.

To cook the chips

Heat the vegetable oil in a deep-fat fryer to 130°C. Cut the potatoes into even-sized pieces and place them in the fryer for 8–9 minutes. Remove the chips and increase the temperature to 180–190°C. Put the chips back in the oil and continue to cook for a further few minutes, until golden.

To prepare the mussels

In a large saucepan, sauté the leek, celery and shallots in butter for about 15 minutes to soften. Add the bay leaves and thyme and continue to cook for another 1–2 minutes. Pour in the white wine and add the mussels. Cover, bring to the boil and cook for 3–4 minutes until the mussels have opened. Stir in the parsley and celery salt and heat through. Discard any unopened mussels.

To serve

Place a spoonful of cabbage on each plate. Add some sea bass on top of the cabbage and sprinkle with a touch of vanilla salt. Add the crispy oysters alongside. Spoon the mussels into a small serving dish and present them on the plate. Finally, arrange the chips in a bowl or dish and garnish with a wedge of lemon and sea salt diamonds.

County chef:
Niall McKenna
Restaurant:
James Street South

Niall McKenna is the owner and head chef at James Street South in the centre of Belfast. He's worked with lots of big names during his career, including Marco Pierre White, Nico Ladenis and Gary Rhodes, but his dream was always to come back to his home town and cook for the people of Belfast.

He opened his restaurant in 2004 and in 2008 it was voted Best Restaurant in Northern Ireland by the Good Food Guide. He likes to cook good simple food with fresh exuberant flavours, and about 90 per cent of the produce he uses is local.

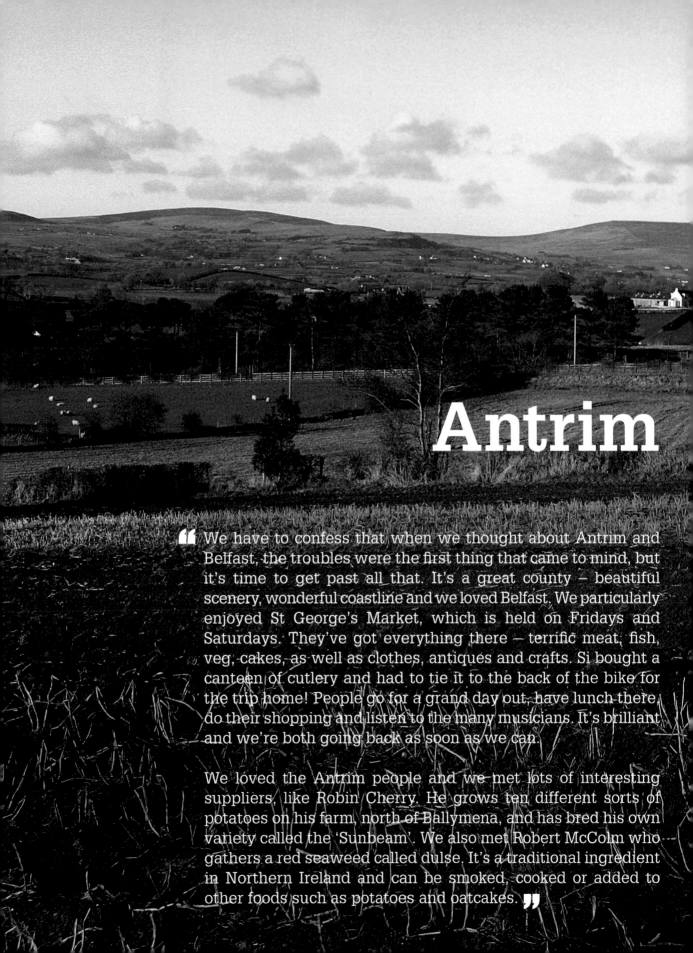

Antrim

"We have to confess that when we thought about Antrim and Belfast, the troubles were the first thing that came to mind, but it's time to get past all that. It's a great county – beautiful scenery, wonderful coastline and we loved Belfast. We particularly enjoyed St George's Market, which is held on Fridays and Saturdays. They've got everything there – terrific meat, fish, veg, cakes, as well as clothes, antiques and crafts. Si bought a canteen of cutlery and had to tie it to the back of the bike for the trip home! People go for a grand day out, have lunch there, do their shopping and listen to the many musicians. It's brilliant and we're both going back as soon as we can.

We loved the Antrim people and we met lots of interesting suppliers, like Robin Cherry. He grows ten different sorts of potatoes on his farm, north of Ballymena, and has bred his own variety called the 'Sunbeam'. We also met Robert McColm who gathers a red seaweed called dulse. It's a traditional ingredient in Northern Ireland and can be smoked, cooked or added to other foods such as potatoes and oatcakes."

The Ulster Fry

Soda bread tastes great and is so quick to make, as you don't need to leave the dough to rise. Eat the bread the same day or fry it up the next. Have a go – it's worth it! And the farls are just the thing to make with left-over mash.

Serves 4

Soda bread
450g plain white flour
1 tsp bicarbonate of soda
1 tsp cream of tartar
1 tsp sea salt, ground to a powder
1 tsp sugar
300ml buttermilk

Potato farls
2 tbsp butter
1kg mashed potatoes
125g plain flour

Fry-up
8 beef or pork sausages
4 tomatoes, cut in half
250–300g button mushrooms
olive oil
8 smoked bacon rashers
8 slices of black pudding
8 eggs
butter

To bake the soda bread
Preheat the oven to 180°C/Gas 4. Sift the flour, bicarb, cream of tartar and salt into a large bowl. Stir in the sugar and then add the buttermilk, and mix together to form a soft dough. If the dough is too dry, add a little more buttermilk or a tablespoonful or 2 of warm water, but take care not to overwork the mixture. Flour your hands and knead the dough very briefly, then shape the dough into a mounded round and place it on a floured baking tray. Cut a deep cross into the top of the loaf. Bake in the middle of the oven for 30–35 minutes, or until the bread sounds hollow when tapped on the bottom.

To cook the fry-up and potato farls
Preheat the oven to 180°C/Gas 4. Arrange the sausages in a baking tin and roast in the oven for 25 minutes, or until they are golden brown and cooked through. Put the tomato halves and button mushrooms in another baking tin, drizzle with olive oil and season with salt and pepper and roast for 10–15 minutes.

to serve:
Put a potato farl on each plate and add the sausages, black pudding, bacon, tomato halves, mushrooms and fried eggs alongside. Slice the soda bread and spread with butter.

Meanwhile, make the potato farls. Melt the butter in a small pan and then mix it into the mashed potatoes, along with a good pinch of salt. Work in the flour and knead lightly on a floured work surface. Divide the mixture into 2 pieces and roll them out on a floured board to make 2 circles the size of a large dinner plate and about 0.5cm thick. Cut into quarters. Heat some vegetable oil in a large non-stick frying pan and fry the farls for 3–4 minutes on each side, until golden brown. Serve warm.

Heat a tablespoon of olive oil in a large non-stick frying pan and fry the black pudding slices for 1–2 minutes on each side. Fry the eggs to your liking.

Niall McKenna's
John Dory
with scallop and mussel nage

Antrim's seafood is stunning and this recipe shows off its flavours beautifully. Don't forget to discard any mussels that don't open.

Serves 4

Nage (fish stock)
700ml water

200ml dry white wine

1 large carrot, 1 large onion, 1 large leek

2 celery sticks

1 bay leaf

3 sprigs of parsley

3 sprigs of thyme

8 peppercorns

1 garlic clove

Cream sauce
fish bones

1 star anise

1 bay leaf

scallop trimmings (skirts)

250ml double cream

¼ garlic clove, finely chopped

juice of 1 lemon

Fish and vegetables
4 baby carrots and 2 baby turnips

4 baby leeks

16 mussels, scrubbed and debearded

12 cherry tomatoes

1 tsp capers

juice of 1 lemon

2 tsp butter

olive oil

2 large John Dory (ask the fishmonger to fillet them but ask for clean bones)

4 large hand-dived scallops

1 tbsp vegetable oil

baby salad leaves

To make the stock
Pour the water and wine into a large saucepan. Roughly chop the carrot, onion, leek and celery and add them to the pan with the bay leaf, parsley, thyme, peppercorns and garlic. Bring to the boil over a medium heat and simmer for 15 minutes. Season with salt and simmer for another 15 minutes. Strain the liquid and divide it into 2 – you need half to cook the mussels and the rest for the creamed foam.

To make the cream sauce
Pour one half of the nage into a pan, add the fish bones, star anise, bay leaf and scallop trimmings and reduce by half over a medium heat. Add the double cream, finely chopped garlic and lemon juice and season with salt and pepper. Taste to check the seasoning and set aside ready to foam with a stick blender before serving.

Ladle a tablespoon of the nage, mussels and vegetables into each bowl. Add a fillet of John Dory on top and a scallop on top of that. Spoon in more of the mussel, nage and vegetables and dress with the baby salad leaves. Whisk the cream sauce into a foam with a stick blender and add a tablespoon to each serving.

Peel and quarter the baby vegetables and cook them in salted, boiling water until al dente. Set aside. Pour the other half of the nage into a large pan, add the cleaned mussels and cook until they open. Discard any that do not open. Add the tomatoes (halved or quartered), capers, half the lemon juice and a teaspoon of butter. Add the al dente vegetables and season with salt, pepper and touch of olive oil.

To cook the John Dory and scallops

Season the fish and scallops (roes removed) with salt and pepper and put them into a hot frying pan with a tablespoon of vegetable oil. Cook for about 2 minutes on one side, then turn them all over and add the scallop roes and a teaspoon of butter. Cook for another 2 minutes, then add the rest of the lemon juice.

Daube of Beef
with colcannon potatoes, best-ever roasties with dulse, and laverbread

Potatoes are really important in Northern Ireland and we had some of the best we've ever eaten there. Treat them with respect and choose the right variety for the dish you're making – ask your greengrocer for different types, not just a bag of whites or reds. We also discovered dulse in Antrim, a seaweed that's often eaten smoked and fried.

Serves 4–6

Daube of beef
2 shins of beef
olive oil
2 tbsp seasoned plain flour
1 carrot, 1 celery stick, 1 onion,
    peeled and finely chopped
2 garlic cloves, crushed
knob of butter
12 baby onions
12 button mushrooms
1 star anise
1 cinnamon stick
bouquet garni (thyme, bay leaves, parsley)
400ml good red wine
50ml Madeira
400ml beef stock
zest and juice of 1 orange
1 tbsp redcurrant jelly

Colcannon
1kg floury spuds, peeled and chopped

1kg spring cabbage, stems removed
    and finely shredded
2 shallots, peeled and sliced
150ml cream
1 tbsp chopped chives
125g butter

Best-ever roasties
loads of good spuds, peeled
    and cut into barrels
180g goose fat
2 tbsp semolina
1 small handful of smoked dulse

Laverbread
400–500ml chicken stock
1 handful of dulse seaweed,
    very finely shredded
vegetable oil
150g unsmoked streaky bacon lardons
knob of butter

To prepare the daube of beef
Preheat the oven to 170°C/Gas 3. Roll both shins of beef and tie them together, thick end to the thin end, to make one stout roll. Tie tightly with butcher's string to make a joint.

Heat 2 tablespoons of olive oil in a large casserole dish. Roll the meat in the seasoned flour and brown all over in the hot olive oil. Set aside.

tip:

Try adding the semolina when roasting your potatoes. It's a trick we learned in Antrim and makes the crispiest potatoes ever. To get the best from potatoes, use varieties that are in season rather than those that have been stored for months.

In the same pan, sweat the carrot, celery and onion for about 5 minutes. Add the garlic and continue to cook for a further minute. Heat 2 more tablespoons of olive oil and a knob of butter in a separate pan and sauté the baby onions and button mushrooms until coloured.

Tip the vegetables into the casserole dish, add the star anise, cinnamon and the bouquet garni. Pour in the red wine, Madeira, beef stock, orange juice and zest. Return the meat to the casserole, along with the sautéed onions and mushrooms. Cover tightly and place in the oven for about 6 hours, until the beef is meltingly soft. Turn the meat every 1½ hours or so.

Once the meat is cooked, remove it from the casserole and leave it to rest for half an hour. Strain the juices from the beef through a sieve into a clean pan and set the vegetables aside. Reduce the juices by half. Stir in the redcurrant jelly and season to taste with sea salt and black pepper, then put the vegetables back in the pan and warm them through. Check the seasoning again.

To make the colcannon

Cook the potatoes in a large pan of salted water, then drain them and mash well. Plunge the shredded cabbage into a separate pan of boiling water and cook until tender. Meanwhile, simmer the shallots, cream and chives for about 5 minutes. Mix this into the potatoes with the cabbage, season well and warm through. Then if your arteries can stand it, top with a puddle of melted butter… yum.

to serve:

Carve the beef into thick slices and arrange on warm plates. Put a serving of veg alongside the beef and spoon over some gravy. Put a spoonful of colcannon next to the beef and dot with a knob of butter and add some roast potatoes, sprinkled with crispy dulse, alongside. Add a small spoonful of laverbread.

To cook the roasties

Preheat the oven to 220°C/Gas 7. Put the potatoes in a large pan of salted water, bring to the boil and cook for 4–5 minutes. Drain well, then put the potatoes back in the pan and shake well to scuff up the surfaces. Melt the goose fat in a roasting tin in the oven. Sprinkle the semolina over the potatoes and tip them into the sizzling fat. Season liberally with sea salt. Cook for 40–45 minutes until the potatoes are really crisp and golden. Put the smoked dulse on a baking tray and dry roast in the oven for 8–10 minutes until crispy. Sprinkle it over the roasties before serving.

To prepare the laverbread

Warm the chicken stock in a pan and add the shredded dulse. Blanch for a few minutes, then drain well. Heat a touch of oil in a frying pan and fry the bacon lardons for 3–4 minutes or until nicely golden. Add the dulse to the bacon and stir in a knob of butter.

County chef:
Clare Johnson
Restaurant:
Kilberry Inn

Clare Johnson is one of Britain's top female chefs and the only female chef in Scotland to hold a Michelin Bib Gourmand. She runs the Kilberry Inn near Loch Fyne with her partner David Wilson and she turns out some of the best food in Argyll.

The Kilberry is a welcoming spot with cosy log fires, and the aim is to provide great food and service in a relaxed, comfortable setting. Clare loves to use the freshest of west coast ingredients, such as mackerel and crab, as well as beef and lamb from local producers.

Argyll & Bute

" This area is simply stunning. We had one of our best motorbike rides ever from Argyll to Dumfries – the scenery is just breathtaking. Including the islands, the county has around 3,000 miles of coastline so it's not surprising that fish and seafood dominate the cooking. It's some of the best in the world. We went out with Big Hughie, the langoustine fisherman, and hauled in 100 pots – Hughie really made us work for our supper! Later, we went to the fishing village of Tarbert on Loch Fyne, an idyllic area where we found so much good seafood, and ate at an amazing restaurant called the Corner House Bistro, run by husband and wife team Pascal and Jacqui. Made friends for life there.

Another great place was the Springbank whisky distillery, the oldest independent distillery in Scotland. This is whisky for the connoisseur, and they still use traditional production methods – the skill involved is remarkable. You'll be glad to know that we got to taste the whisky, which is extraordinarily good, and we noticed a link between the product and the environment. The whisky is produced right next to the sea and there is a salty tang to the taste. You couldn't make Springbank anywhere else. "

Fried Fish in Oatmeal
with tartare sauce

This is a traditional way of cooking herring – the oatmeal gives great texture to the fish. The day we were cooking this for the mobile kitchen we found a fellow down a backstreet selling all kinds of good fish. We bought what he had so we could try the oatmeal coating with other fish and make a kind of Scottish fritto misto.

Serves 4

600g fish fillets
   (herring, smoked haddock, plaice)
juice of ½ lemon
4 tbsp flour
2 eggs, beaten
200g pinhead oatmeal
sunflower oil for frying
lemon wedges

Quick tartare sauce

1 x 500g jar of good mayonnaise
2 tbsp chopped capers
2 tbsp chopped cornichons or gherkins
2 tbsp chopped parsley
2 tbsp chopped dill
juice of ½ lemon
a good dash of Tabasco

Remove any bones from the fish fillets and cut them into goujons (thin strips). Dress with a squeeze of lemon. Season the flour with salt and pepper. Dredge each piece of fish in flour, dip in beaten egg and then coat in pinhead oatmeal.

Mix together all the ingredients for the tartare sauce and check the seasoning. Put it into a bowl ready to serve and set aside.

tip:
Don't be too set in your ideas when shopping for fish – go for what looks best on the day. Look at the fish carefully, checking that the gills are red and the eyes bright. If it doesn't look fresh, don't buy it.

Heat a large frying pan and pour in enough oil to cover the bottom of the pan. Once the oil is hot, cook the pieces of fish in batches until they are crispy and cooked through. Turn them carefully so they don't break up. Drain each batch on kitchen paper and keep warm while you cook the rest.

To serve
Sprinkle the goujons with sea salt and serve with lemon wedges and the bowl of tartare sauce.

Clare Johnson's
Hand-dived Scallops
with spiced sausage balls,
puy lentils and salsa verde

**When cooking scallops, make sure the pan is blisteringly hot before you put
in the scallops – you want them to sear, not poach. A cast-iron pan is perfect
for this job. Once the scallops are in the frying pan, don't move them until the
underside is caramelised.**

Serves 4

5–7 scallops per person,
  depending on the size
olive oil

Lentils
100g puy lentils
500ml vegetable stock
2 bay leaves
1 sprig of thyme
1 onion, finely chopped
1 carrot, finely diced
1 celery stick, finely diced
olive oil

Salsa verde
1 large handful of parsley
1 handful of basil
1 tsp Dijon mustard
1 garlic clove
150–250ml olive oil
½ red onion, finely chopped
1 tbsp baby capers

Spiced sausage balls
250g good sausage meat
½ tsp cayenne pepper
1 tsp fennel seeds
vegetable oil

To cook the lentils
Rinse the lentils well under cold water. Put them into a pan and add the stock, bay
leaves and thyme and cook for 20–25 minutes until tender. Sauté the finely chopped
onion, carrot and celery in a little olive oil. Once the lentils are cooked, drain them and
mix with the sautéed vegetables. Season to taste.

To prepare the salsa verde
Wash the herbs well and put them into a food processor with the mustard and garlic.
Add some olive oil and whizz everything to make a sauce. Pour into a bowl and mix
in the red onion and capers. Stir a spoonful or 2 into the lentils and set the rest aside.

To make the spiced sausage balls

Mix the sausage meat with the cayenne pepper and fennel seeds, then season. Roll into small, walnut-sized balls. Heat some vegetable oil in a frying pan and fry the sausage balls over a medium heat until cooked through.

tip:
Oil the scallops,
not the pan.

To cook the scallops

Heat a frying pan until blisteringly hot. Brush the scallops with oil, then sear quickly until caramelised and crispy on the outside and soft in the middle (no more than a minute is required on each side).

To serve

Put a mound of lentils in the middle of a plate, add the sausage balls and scallops

Langoustines Flamed in Whisky Sauce

with potato cakes, quails' egg tempura and wilted spinach

We went fishing for langoustines while we were up in Argyll. We hauled in the pots from the crystal-clear water and we've never tasted sweeter seafood. Treat your langoustines with respect and take care not to overcook them – you'll enjoy a delicious feast.

Serves 4–6

Dill and lemon potato cakes

500g waxy potatoes
1 egg, beaten
1 tbsp finely chopped dill
zest of ½ lemon
1 tsp fresh lemon juice
3 tbsp olive oil

Quails' egg tempura

8 quails' eggs
1 tbsp celery salt
1 tbsp ground black pepper
70g plain flour
60g cornflour
1 tsp baking powder
1 tsp bicarbonate of soda
100ml iced sparkling water
1 egg, beaten
vegetable oil for frying

Grilled langoustines

8 langoustines, split down the middle
2 garlic cloves, crushed
50g butter, softened

Sautéed langoustines

1kg langoustines
25g unsalted butter
1 tbsp olive oil
2 tsp malt whisky
2 tbsp crème fraîche
1 tbsp chopped parsley

Spinach

500g baby spinach, stalks removed
knob of butter
freshly grated nutmeg

To make the potato cakes

Boil the potatoes in their skins for 5 minutes – they are only meant to be partly cooked – and allow to cool. Peel the potatoes, then grate them into a large bowl. Mix in the egg, dill, lemon zest and juice and a tablespoon of olive oil, then season with salt and black pepper.

Heat the remaining oil in a frying pan. Place a tablespoon of the potato mixture into the pan and flatten with a spatula. Repeat until you have 4 on the go. Cook until golden, then turn and cook on the other side. Keep warm until ready to serve.

To make the quails' egg tempura

Boil the eggs for precisely 2 minutes, then plunge them into ice-cold water to stop the cooking process. Carefully peel the eggs, making sure the membrane comes off with the shell, then blot them on kitchen paper. Mix the celery salt with the black pepper and carefully roll the eggs in this seasoning.

To make the tempura batter, mix the plain flour and cornflour together and add the baking powder and bicarb. Add the sparkling mineral water to the beaten egg. Fold the watery egg mixture into the flour to make a runny batter. Don't mix this too much – some lumpy, floury bits are fine.

Heat the oil to a gentle rumble in a deep-fat fryer – about 170°C. Using your fingers, carefully dip each egg into the tempura batter and roll it around until well coated. Drop the eggs into the hot oil and cook for 90 seconds until golden. Take care not to overcook. Remove and drain on kitchen paper. Ideally, cook the tempura at the last moment and serve immediately.

To cook the langoustines and spinach

Place the split langoustines on a grill pan. Mix the crushed garlic and softened butter together and smear it over the flesh. Season with sea salt and ground black pepper and grill until just cooked.

To prepare the sautéed langoustines, first blanch them for 2 minutes in boiling water, then plunge them straight into ice-cold water before peeling them. Heat the butter and olive oil in a large frying pan. Add the shelled langoustines and cook for about 3 minutes. Pour in the whisky and flambé for a minute or so. Then add the crème fraîche and parsley and check the seasoning.

Wilt the spinach in a big pan with a knob of butter. Drain well, then chop lightly, season and top with some grated nutmeg.

To serve

Place a potato cake on each warm plate and top with an egg. Place a spoonful of the sautéed langoustines to one side and some spinach. Add 2 grilled langoustines on the top and gently pour over the whisky sauce.

County chef:
Sue Manson and Maryann Wright
Restaurant:
Y Polyn

Y Polynn is one of only two restaurants in Camarthenshire recommended by the Michelin Guide. It is run by two couples – Sue and Maryann head the kitchen and their husbands, Simon and Mark, look after the front of house. They aim to serve good food at reasonable prices in a relaxed setting and their seasonal menu is a sensitive blend of pub and fine dining classics. They use local produce whenever possible and make everything on site, including ice cream and excellent bread.

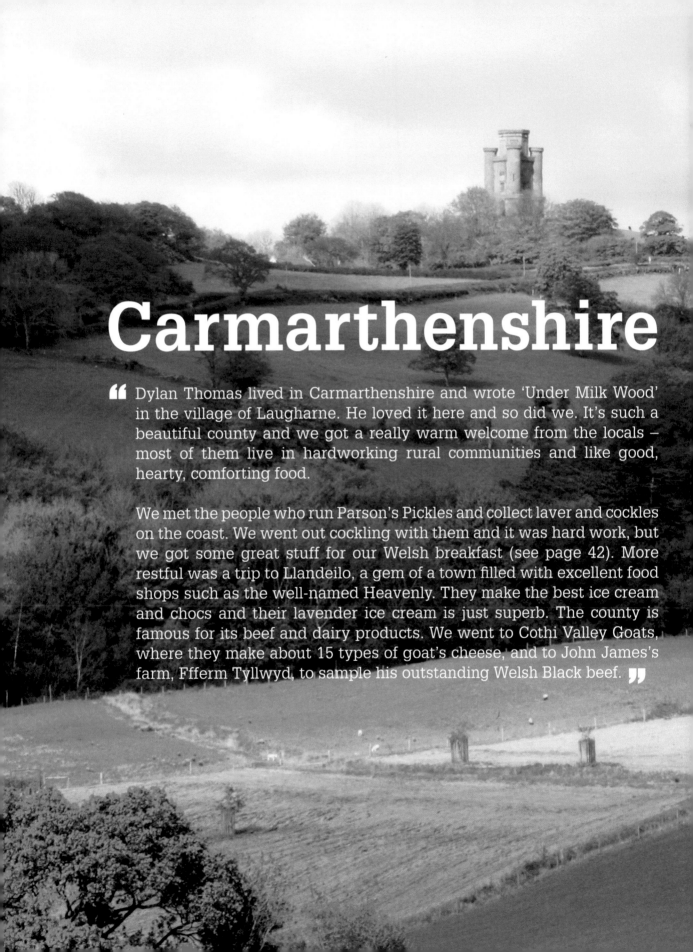

Carmarthenshire

" Dylan Thomas lived in Carmarthenshire and wrote 'Under Milk Wood' in the village of Laugharne. He loved it here and so did we. It's such a beautiful county and we got a really warm welcome from the locals — most of them live in hardworking rural communities and like good, hearty, comforting food.

We met the people who run Parson's Pickles and collect laver and cockles on the coast. We went out cockling with them and it was hard work, but we got some great stuff for our Welsh breakfast (see page 42). More restful was a trip to Llandeilo, a gem of a town filled with excellent food shops such as the well-named Heavenly. They make the best ice cream and chocs and their lavender ice cream is just superb. The county is famous for its beef and dairy products. We went to Cothi Valley Goats, where they make about 15 types of goat's cheese, and to John James's farm, Ffferm Tyllwyd, to sample his outstanding Welsh Black beef. **"**

Cockles, Laverbread and Welsh Bacon

This combination is traditionally known as a Welsh breakfast and was something we wanted to try in our mobile kitchen. Laver is a kind of seaweed which is cooked and puréed to make laverbread, a Welsh delicacy.

Serves 4

225g cockles (meat only), cleaned, cooked and shelled
225g laverbread, ready prepared
50g oatmeal
freshly ground white pepper
25g butter
1 medium leek, finely chopped
50g bacon fat
8 rashers of smoked bacon

First soak the cockles in fresh water to get rid of any sand and throw out any that have broken shells. Steam them for a couple of minutes in a large pan, then remove the flesh. Discard any that don't open.

Mix the laverbread with the oatmeal and a good grinding of white pepper. Leave to stand for 20 minutes. Heat a frying pan, add the butter and sauté the leek until soft. Add the cockles and cook until warmed through, then set aside.

Heat the bacon fat in a pan. With slightly wet hands, shape the laverbread mix into pieces about the size of a golf ball and flatten them down slightly to make small patties. Fry them in the bacon fat until slightly crispy on both sides and keep warm. Quickly sauté the bacon until crispy and cooked.

To serve
Serve the laverbread patties with the cockles, leeks and bacon.

Sue Manson and Maryann Wright's Braised Beef Cheek

with crispy ox tongue and stir-fry of Carmarthen bacon

You need to think ahead for this recipe and start the night before you want to eat it, as both meats need marinating.

Serves 4

Beef cheeks

4 beef cheeks, about 375g each

bottle of red wine

2 carrots, peeled and cut into chunks

1 large onion, peeled and quartered

4 celery sticks, cut into chunks

1 medium leek

4 garlic cloves

4 bay leaves

1 sprig of thyme

10 black peppercorns

1 star anise

olive oil

1 tsp tomato purée

1 tsp plain flour

Ox tongue

thyme leaves

1 small tongue, about 500g

duck fat

1 egg, beaten

Japanese panko breadcrumbs

vegetable oil

Stir-fry

½ medium onion, finely diced

butter

110g Carmarthen bacon, cut into lardons

1 head of spring greens, finely shredded

honey to taste

Parsnip mash

4 medium parsnips, peeled

4 floury potatoes, peeled

110g butter, melted

To prepare the beef cheeks

Trim the cheeks, removing any membrane and excess fat, until you are left with lean pieces of fleshy meat. Tie these up into neat parcels using 2 or 3 pieces of butcher's string. Cover with the wine, add the vegetables, herbs and spices, and leave to marinate overnight in the fridge.

The next day, sear the meat in olive oil until browned and place in a heavy casserole dish. Lightly brown the marinated vegetables in the same pan you used to sear the meat. Add the tomato purée and flour to the browned vegetables and cook for about a minute. Then add the cooked vegetables to the casserole, tucking them around the meat, and season. Pour in the marinade wine and top up with more red wine to cover if necessary. Bring this to the boil, cover and place in a low oven at 140°C/Gas 1 for at least 6 hours. Check the liquid every hour to make sure the meat is still submerged and add a little water if needed.

Remove the casserole from the oven and leave the meat to cool in the liquid with the lid off. Strain the liquid and reserve, discarding the vegetables. Take the string off the meat. When almost ready to serve, heat the meat in half the liquid and put it back into a low oven for 20 minutes. Make the red wine sauce by bringing the rest of the liquid to the boil and reducing until glossy and thick.

To cook the crispy ox tongue

Mix a generous amount of salt and pepper with the thyme leaves and coat the tongue with the mix. Leave overnight in the fridge.

The next day, melt the duck fat in a saucepan and place the tongue in a small baking tray – it should be a snug fit. Pour the duck fat over the tongue, completely covering it, and then cover with a sheet of baking parchment and tuck a sheet of foil over the top, sealing it tightly. Cook the tongue in a low oven at 140°C/Gas 1 for 2 hours. Leave to cool and then remove the tongue from the fat and chill in the fridge.

After 30 minutes or so, remove the outer skin from the tongue and cut it into chunks about 2cm thick. Coat in beaten egg and panko breadcrumbs. When you are ready to serve, heat some oil to 180°C in a deep-fat fryer and fry the tongue for around 3 minutes (at this temperature a piece of bread dropped in will sizzle and brown in 30 seconds).

To make the stir-fry

Sweat the onion in a little butter until soft. Gently cook the bacon lardons in a dry, non-stick pan. Combine the onions and bacon in a large pan, add the spring greens and cook over a low heat until the greens wilt. Drizzle with honey to taste and season with freshly milled pepper and a little salt – be sparing as the bacon is salty.

To make the parsnip mash

Cook the parsnips and potatoes in salted water until tender, then dry them out in a warm pan. Pass through a potato ricer. Add the melted butter and beat together until light and smooth. Season to taste.

To serve

Place the meat parcels on the plates and pour the red wine sauce over them. Add some crispy ox tongue next to the meat with some parsnip mash to the side and serve the stir-fry in a separate dish.

Welsh Black Beef Wellington
with goat's cheese, garlic and chervil mash, and beer gravy

This is a very special beef and it tastes amazing made into beef Wellington – slice and smile! We liked the idea of combining this with another great local food – goat's cheese.

Serves 8

Beer gravy
50g unsalted butter
½ tbsp brown sugar
4 onions, finely chopped
250ml good beef stock
1 tsp mustard powder
250ml strong beer or stout

Pancakes
120g plain flour
1 large egg, beaten
300ml full-fat milk
1 tbsp melted butter
2 tsp chopped parsley
1 tsp chopped thyme
1 tsp chopped chervil
extra knob of butter

Duxelles
100g unsalted butter
3 shallots, finely chopped
500g mushrooms,
    finely chopped
15g dried porcini mushrooms,
    soaked in a little boiling water
1 tbsp double cream

1 tbsp chopped parsley
1 egg white

Beef Wellington
1kg centre-cut fillet of Welsh black beef
1 tbsp vegetable oil
1 packet of puff pastry
1 egg, beaten

Goat's cheese, garlic and chervil mash
2 tbsp melted butter
2 garlic cloves, lightly crushed
1kg good floury potatoes
2 tbsp double cream
100g goat's cheese,
    cut into small cubes
1 tbsp chopped fresh chervil

Broad beans, lettuce and shallots
50g butter
2 shallots, finely chopped
500g broad beans, podded, blanched
    and skinned
150ml chicken stock
4 baby gem lettuces

tip:
The pancakes in this beef Wellington help stop the pastry going soggy and also add texture.

To make the beer gravy

First let's get the gravy going. Melt the butter and stir in the sugar. Add the onions and cook slowly until they are very brown and caramelised. Add the stock, mustard powder and beer. Season well with salt and pepper, then simmer until it is reduced by half.

To make the pancakes

Season the flour with sea salt and black pepper and add the beaten egg. Gradually add the milk, whisking continuously to make a smooth batter. Add the melted butter and chopped herbs and leave to stand for at least 20 minutes. Heat a good non-stick pan and melt a little butter. Add a spoonful of batter to cover the bottom of the pan. Cook until golden, then flip and cook the other side. Repeat until all the batter is used. Cut the pancakes into squares, lay flat on silicon paper on an oven tray and set aside.

To make the duxelles

Melt the butter in a large frying pan, add the shallots and cook until soft. Add the mushrooms, cover the pan and cook for another 5 minutes. Drain the porcini, chop them finely and add them to the mushroom mix, then add the porcini soaking juices and the cream. Stir and cook with the lid off until the juices have evaporated. Leave to cool. Stir in the parsley and the egg white, then place in a food processor and blitz. Don't make it too fine – it should have some texture. Spread the mushroom duxelles on to the pancakes and chill until the mushrooms have set.

To prepare the beef Wellington

Preheat the oven to 180°C/Gas 4. Rub the beef with sea salt flakes and ground black pepper. Heat the vegetable oil in a frying pan until it's smoking. Sear the fillet all over, including the ends, and then set aside to cool. Carefully roll out the puff pastry quite thinly to make a rectangular shape. Place the duxelles-coated pancakes on to the pastry, mushroom side up. Cut them to fit as necessary, but leave a border around the edge for sealing. Lay the seared beef fillet on top and fold the pastry around the meat. Brush the edges with beaten egg and seal the pastry snugly round the meat, then make a couple of small holes in the pastry casing to let the steam escape. Put on to a baking sheet and bake in the oven for about 30 minutes until the pastry is golden. This will give you medium-rare beef, which is what we go for.

To make the mash

Heat the butter until it's hot but not bubbling and add the lightly crushed garlic. Leave it to steep in the butter for half an hour at least. Peel the potatoes and cut into even-sized chunks. Poach them in salted boiling water until tender – poaching gives better results than boiling when cooking potatoes for mash. Drain the potatoes and put them back in the pan. Place the pan on top of the oven so the potatoes can dry out for a few minutes. Mash the potatoes until smooth. Beat in the cream, goat's cheese and garlicky butter, then fold in the chopped chervil and season to taste.

To cook the vegetables

Melt the butter in a frying pan and soften the shallots. Add the broad beans and chicken stock. Finely shred the baby gem lettuces and once the beans are cooked through, fold in the lettuce.

To serve

Place a couple of healthy slices of the beef Wellington on each plate. Serve with the mash and broad beans on the side with a drizzle of beer gravy.

County chef:
David Mooney
Restaurant:
Belle Epoque

A firm favourite in the area, Belle Epoque in Knutsford has been run by the Mooney family for 36 years. David is head chef, his brother Matthew looks after front of house and their mother is at the restaurant several nights a week. Before joining the family business, David worked with some of Britain's best chefs, including Raymond Blanc and Marco Pierre White. The restaurant has been voted Cheshire Life Restaurant of the Year among other accolades, but David is more concerned with pleasing his customers with good food than winning awards. He describes his food as Modern British and he and his brother pride themselves on sourcing all their produce within 50 miles of the restaurant.

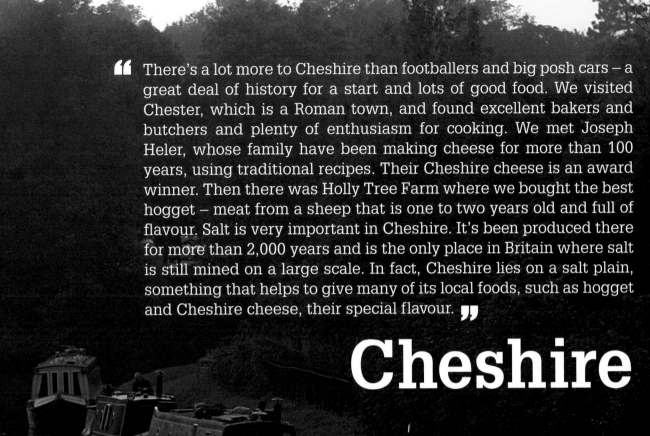

“ There's a lot more to Cheshire than footballers and big posh cars – a great deal of history for a start and lots of good food. We visited Chester, which is a Roman town, and found excellent bakers and butchers and plenty of enthusiasm for cooking. We met Joseph Heler, whose family have been making cheese for more than 100 years, using traditional recipes. Their Cheshire cheese is an award winner. Then there was Holly Tree Farm where we bought the best hogget – meat from a sheep that is one to two years old and full of flavour. Salt is very important in Cheshire. It's been produced there for more than 2,000 years and is the only place in Britain where salt is still mined on a large scale. In fact, Cheshire lies on a salt plain, something that helps to give many of its local foods, such as hogget and Cheshire cheese, their special flavour. ”

Cheshire

Cheshire Soup
with fried Cheshire cheese sarnies

This soup is a local recipe and handy for using up odds and ends of cheese. We found out that Cheshire cheese is one of the oldest known in Britain and is even referred to in the Domesday Book.

Serves 6–8

Soup

1.5 litres chicken stock

3 large potatoes, peeled and diced

4 carrots, peeled and grated

4 leeks, halved lengthways, finely sliced

6 tbsp quick-cook oats

400g Cheshire cheese
   (white and blue mixed), grated

Garnish

½ leek, finely sliced

1 small bunch of watercress,

Sarnies

110g butter, softened

1 loaf white bread, thinly sliced

300g Cheshire cheese, thinly sliced

3 tbsp olive oil

tip:

Quick-cook oats make this soup a bit more substantial. In fact, they make a good thickening agent for many types of soup and stew.

To prepare the soup

Pour the stock into a large pan and bring it to the boil. Add the potatoes and simmer for 5 minutes, then add the carrots and leeks and simmer for another 5 minutes. Add the oats and cook for 5 minutes. Using a potato masher, mash the vegetables in the pan.

Add the cheese and check the seasoning. Cook for another few minutes, then ladle into bowls and garnish with a few slices of leek and some watercress leaves.

To make the sarnies

Butter the bread. Layer cheese over half the slices, then top with the remaining slices of bread to make sandwiches. Cut off the crusts and cut each sandwich in half.

Heat a frying pan until medium hot, then add the olive oil and some of the remaining butter. Fry the sandwiches for 1–2 minutes until golden brown and the cheese is starting to melt, then flip and cook on the other side until equally golden. Remove from the pan and cut into squares to serve with the soup.

David Mooney's Arley Wild Boar

with winter preserved plums and dauphinoise potatoes

Wild boar is a delicious lean meat and much easier to get hold of these days. If you can't get wild boar, use a good, rare-breed pork, such as Berkshire Black.

Serves 4

75g carrot, celery and onion, finely chopped
olive oil
110g butter
4 preserved plums, chopped, plus syrup
125ml red wine (drinkable quality!)
400ml boar or pork stock
2 tenderloins of wild boar
200g wild boar liver
200g carrots, cut into small batons
1 tbsp caster sugar

400g baby spinach leaves, washed and picked

Dauphinoise potatoes

6 large potatoes, peeled and thinly sliced
200g strong Cheddar cheese, grated
4 garlic cloves, finely chopped
250ml double cream

To prepare the dauphinoise potatoes

Preheat the oven to 150°C/Gas 2. Layer the potatoes, cheese, garlic, salt and pepper into an ovenproof dish, finishing with cheese on the top. Pour in the cream until it is just visible, cover with foil and cook for 3 hours. When cooked, cut into portions.

To prepare the wild boar

Preheat the oven to 220°C/Gas 7. Sauté the carrots, celery and onion with a little oil and some of the butter and sweat down. Add the syrup from the plums and the red wine and cook until the liquid is reduced. Add the stock and cook until reduced once more, season and strain. Add the chopped plums, then set the sauce aside and keep it warm.

Heat an ovenproof frying pan until smoking and add a little butter. Seal the boar tenderloins on each side, then place in the hot oven for 6–8 minutes. Remove and leave to rest for 5 minutes. Place the frying pan back on the heat, add a little more butter and cook the boar liver on each side for 1 minute. Remove and leave to rest.

Heat a separate frying pan until hot, add some more butter and the carrots and sauté for 1–2 minutes. Add the sugar, toss to combine, then place in the oven and roast for 5–10 minutes until tender. Heat another frying pan until hot, add the last of the butter and the spinach and swirl around, until wilted. Remove and drain on kitchen paper.

to serve:
Cutting at an angle, carve the boar and the liver into slices. Pile some carrots on each plate and top with the spinach. Lay a few slices of wild boar on top. Place some dauphinoise alongside, add a piece of liver and spoon the sauce and plums over and around.

Spiced Hogget
with swede and
Cheshire cheese gâteau

When making the swede and cheese gâteau you will need eight chef's rings of the size you want the gâteau to be. You will also need a cutter just a tiny bit smaller than the chef's rings.

Serves 8

Hogget

2 tbsp olive oil

110g speck or fatty smoked bacon,
    finely diced

2 onions, finely diced

1.25kg trimmed shoulder of hogget,
    cut into cubes

200ml red wine

300ml chicken stock

2 garlic cloves, crushed

6 anchovies

20 capers

zest of 1 lemon

1 tsp ground cumin

½ tsp ground ginger

1 tsp ground coriander

4cm cinnamon stick

2 bay leaves

2 tsp fresh thyme leaves

2 sage leaves, chopped

2 tsp chopped fresh rosemary

4 tbsp roughly chopped
    flat-leaf parsley

Swede and Cheshire cheese gâteau

1 bulb of smoked garlic

1 tsp olive oil

600g swede, very finely sliced

2 tbsp plain flour

1 tsp salt

1 tsp ground white pepper

1 tsp ground coriander

110g butter

150g Cheshire cheese, cut into thin slices

175ml single cream

To prepare the hogget

Preheat the oven to 160°C/Gas 3. Heat the oil in a large casserole dish, add the chopped speck or streaky bacon and fry until golden. Then add the diced onions and cook until translucent. Add the meat and cook until browned, then add the wine and stock and bring to a simmer. Add the garlic, anchovies, capers, lemon zest, spices, bay leaves, thyme, sage and rosemary to the casserole, cover and bring to the boil.

Place the dish in the oven and cook for 1½–2 hours, checking and stirring occasionally. Add some more red wine if the mixture starts to look dry. If the meat is not very tender at the end of the cooking time, place the casserole on the hob and simmer for up to 1 hour, checking the liquid every so often. Before serving, stir in the chopped parsley.

tip:

Because hogget comes from older animals, it has richer, deeper flavour than lamb and a good marbling of fat. It's a great meat to use in curries, such as saag gosht.

To prepare the Cheshire cheese gâteau

Preheat the oven to 160°C/Gas 3. Cut the top off the garlic bulb, place it on a sheet of foil, drizzle over the oil and place in the oven for 30 minutes. Using the cutter, cut out circles of swede. You will need about 5 discs per gâteau. Place the flour, salt, pepper and ground coriander in a plastic bag, add the discs of swede and shake until they are covered with seasoned flour.

Put the chef's rings for the gâteau on a baking tray and line each ring with foil. Place a disc of baking parchment at the bottom of each ring, then line the sides with baking parchment as well.

Remove the garlic from the oven and squeeze the flesh into a saucepan with the butter and mash together. Once mashed, place the pan on the heat until the butter has melted. Paint the parchment in each ring with the melted garlic butter. Place a swede disc in the bottom of each ring, then alternate 4 more discs with slices of Cheshire cheese, finishing with a cheese layer. Dot with butter and fill up each ring with cream.

to serve:

Serve the hogget on warm plates with a swede and Cheshire cheese gâteau alongside.

Place in the oven for 45–60 minutes until the tops are golden and the swede is cooked through. Check halfway through the cooking time – if the tops are cooking quicker than the swede, cover with foil for the last part of the cooking. Take out of the oven and leave to cool slightly. Remove the rings and ease each gâteau from its foil – you can tidy up the sides with a knife.

County chef:
Kevin Viner
Restaurant:
Viners

Viners is set in glorious countryside within easy reach of Padstow, Newquay and the Eden project. It's a converted country pub and has a comfortable farmhouse feel. Chef-proprietor Kevin describes his approach in three words: honest, sincere and local, and it's certainly working. He's been awarded a Michelin Bib Gourmand and also holds three AA rosettes. Kevin sources the best local produce and is constantly changing his menu to make the best use of seasonal ingredients. He also serves a local roast rib of beef every Sunday lunchtime.

I love em Mum!

BEEFBURGERS
SAUSAGES
HOGS PUDDING

Freshly made every day!

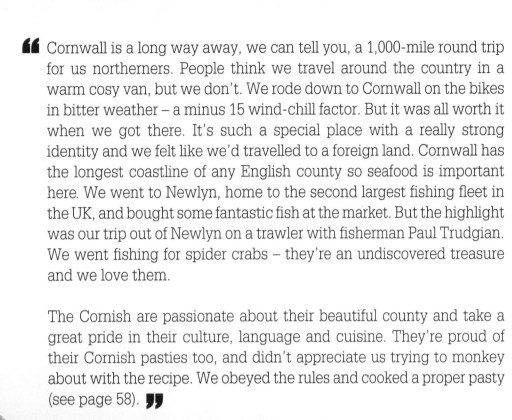

"Cornwall is a long way away, we can tell you, a 1,000-mile round trip for us northerners. People think we travel around the country in a warm cosy van, but we don't. We rode down to Cornwall on the bikes in bitter weather – a minus 15 wind-chill factor. But it was all worth it when we got there. It's such a special place with a really strong identity and we felt like we'd travelled to a foreign land. Cornwall has the longest coastline of any English county so seafood is important here. We went to Newlyn, home to the second largest fishing fleet in the UK, and bought some fantastic fish at the market. But the highlight was our trip out of Newlyn on a trawler with fisherman Paul Trudgian. We went fishing for spider crabs – they're an undiscovered treasure and we love them.

The Cornish are passionate about their beautiful county and take a great pride in their culture, language and cuisine. They're proud of their Cornish pasties too, and didn't appreciate us trying to monkey about with the recipe. We obeyed the rules and cooked a proper pasty (see page 58)."

Cornwall

The People's Cornish Pasty

Feelings run high about pasties in Cornwall. People love them and don't believe in tinkering with the traditional recipe. This is what we learned. Always use beef skirt, nothing fancy. Don't blanch the veg – put them in raw. Don't include carrots and don't use herbs – just lots of black pepper.

Serves 6

Pasty

450g plain flour
2 tsp baking powder
1 tsp salt
125g unsalted butter
2 egg yolks
125ml cold water

Filling

450g potatoes, finely diced
150g swede, finely diced
150g onions, finely chopped
salt and black pepper
300g beef skirt, finely chopped
1 tbsp plain flour
40g butter
1 egg, beaten

To make the pastry

Place the flour, baking powder, salt, butter and egg yolks into a food processor and blitz until the mixture forms crumbs. Slowly add the water until a ball of pastry miraculously appears – you may not need all the water. Wrap the pastry in clingfilm and leave it to chill in the fridge for an hour.

To prepare the filling

Preheat the oven to 180°C/Gas 4. Roll out the pastry to the thickness you like, but be careful not to tear it. Using a dinner plate as a template, cut out 6 discs of pastry. Season the vegetables separately with salt and black pepper. Put the beef into a bowl and mix with the flour and some salt and pepper.

Place some potatoes, swede, onions and beef on one half of the circle, leaving a gap round the edge. Dot with butter. Brush around the perimeter of the pastry circle with the beaten egg, then fold the pastry over the vegetables and meat and seal firmly. Starting at one side, crimp the edges over to form a sealed D-shaped pasty. Brush the whole pasty with beaten egg, then make a steam hole in the centre with a sharp knife. Repeat to make the other pasties.

Put the pasties in the oven and cook for 50 minutes until they are crispy and golden and the filling is cooked through. Leave them to rest for 5–10 minutes before eating.

the pasty's past:
People have probably been making pasties since the 13th century, but it was in the 18th century that they really became popular as a convenient meal for miners and farm workers to take with them to work. The size and shape makes the pasty easy to carry and the sturdy pastry makes a great edible lunchbox.

Kevin Viner's Fillet of Monkfish in Cornish Wine

with pickled celeriac and cucumber

The pickled celeriac is wonderful with the fish, but Kevin says it is also great with a ham sandwich for lunch.

Serves 4

Monkfish

375ml Camel Valley red wine
1 garlic clove, chopped
1 shallot, chopped
1 sprig of thyme
1 sprig of flat-leaf parsley
1 bay leaf
500ml fish stock or water
200g seaweed or sea lettuce
500g monkfish, skinned and filleted
melted butter and lemon juice
truffle oil

Celeriac and cucumber

1 celeriac
zest and juice of 1 lemon
sea salt and white pepper
1 pinch of saffron
250ml white wine
75ml extra virgin olive oil
1 cucumber
50g red seedless grapes

Red wine sauce

375ml Camel Valley red wine
150ml veal or chicken stock
1 shallot, chopped
1 garlic clove, chopped
1 sprig of thyme

Beurre blanc

375ml Camel Valley
sparkling white wine
¼ garlic clove, chopped
1 shallot, chopped
75g unsalted butter

To prepare the monkfish

Put the wine, garlic, shallot, herbs and stock or water into a saucepan, bring to a simmer and cook for 5 minutes. Add the seaweed and bring back to simmer. Turn the heat very low, add the monkfish and poach gently for 10 minutes. To check if the fish is cooked, place a knife or skewer into the centre of a fillet, then remove and hold it against your lower lip. If the knife or skewer feels hot, you know the fish is cooked all the way through.

Drain the fish well and brush it with some melted butter and a squeeze of lemon juice. Carve into slices, allowing 3 per person. Brush over with more butter or even a little truffle oil before serving.

To prepare the pickled celeriac and cucumber

Peel the celeriac, cut it into thin strips and place them in a heat-proof bowl. Put the lemon, salt, pepper, saffron, 200ml of the white wine and the olive oil into a saucepan and bring to the boil. Pour this mixture over the celeriac strips and leave to soak for 2 hours, turning occasionally.

Peel the cucumber and cut the flesh into ribbons with a peeler – don't use the seeded part of the cucumber. Slice the red grapes in half and remove the seeds if necessary. Warm the cucumber in a pan with the remaining 50ml of white wine. Drain the celeriac and toss it with the drained cucumber and sliced grapes.

To make the red wine sauce

Put all the ingredients in a saucepan and heat until the liquid is reduced and syrupy. Strain through a sieve into a clean saucepan.

To make the beurre blanc

Put all the ingredients, except the butter, into a saucepan. Heat until the liquid is reduced and has a syrupy consistency. Whisk in the butter at the end to make the sauce and then strain through a sieve into a clean saucepan.

To serve

Put the warm celeriac and cucumber on to hot plates. Add the monkfish slices, brushed with oil or butter, on top. Lightly reheat under a grill but do not overheat. Circle the sauces around the outside of the plate, first the beurre blanc and then the red wine sauce.

Spider Crab, Lemon and Lemon Thyme Risotto
with tea-smoked scallops, pan-fried grey mullet, spinach and beurre noisette

It's quite tricky to pick out the meat from spider crabs as it's all in the legs, but it's worth it. Grey mullet, also known as silver mullet, is as tasty as sea bass.

Serves 4

Risotto
1 litre chicken stock
25g butter
1 tbsp olive oil
1 onion, finely chopped
2 garlic cloves, roughly chopped
250g risotto rice
zest and juice of 1 lemon
2 sprigs of thyme,
   leaves roughly chopped
50ml double cream
2 tbsp Pecorino cheese,
   freshly grated
250g fresh white crab meat

Tea-smoked scallops
8 hand-dived scallops,
   cleaned and shelled
1 tbsp olive oil
50g demerara sugar
50g long-grain rice
20g English tea or Lapsang Souchong

Mullet and spinach
110g unsalted butter
juice of 1 lemon
2 tbsp capers
2 tbsp finely chopped parsley
2 large fillets of grey mullet
2 tbsp olive oil
1 small bag of baby spinach leaves

tip:
For our tea-smoked scallops we used Tregothnan tea, which is grown in Cornwall. Tea has been grown on the Tregothnan Estate for 200 years and it is the only commercial tea producer in Britain.

To prepare the risotto
Bring the chicken stock to a simmer in a saucepan. Heat a separate pan, add the butter, olive oil, onion and garlic and sweat for 2–3 minutes until the onion is just softened. Add the rice and stir well to coat the rice in butter. Add the lemon zest and juice and stir well.

Reduce the heat to low, then start to add the stock, a ladleful at a time, stirring well in between each addition. Let each ladleful be fully absorbed before adding any more. Cook for 25–30 minutes until the rice is tender and all the stock is absorbed. Add the thyme, double cream and cheese and stir well, then season with salt and black pepper. Finally, stir in the crab meat and adjust the seasoning once more.

To prepare the tea-smoked scallops

Thread the scallops on to skewers and brush them with olive oil. (If you're using wooden skewers, make sure you soak them in water first.) Fold a large piece of foil into 4 and place it in the bottom of a wok, then pour the sugar, rice and tea on to the foil.

Set a rack across the top of the wok and rest the skewers of scallops on the rack. Season the scallops with a little salt and black pepper. Place the wok over a very low heat and cook for about 15–20 minutes. The scallops will be smoky in colour and just cooked through.

To prepare the mullet and spinach

to serve:

Using a chef's ring, make a neat pile of the risotto on one side of the plate. Slice the scallops finely and place on top of the risotto. Add a bed of spinach. Top with a piece of fish, skin side up, and pour the reheated beurre noisette over the fish.

First make the beurre noisette by placing three-quarters of the butter into a frying pan and heating it until it goes nut brown in colour. Add the lemon juice, capers and parsley – this stops the cooking process. Set the butter aside to be reheated later.

Season the fish and slash the skin to stop the fillets curling while cooking. Heat the oil in a frying pan and put in the fish, skin side down. This will be the presentation side so wait until the skin has turned crisp and golden-brown in colour. Carefully turn the fish on to the flesh side for the last couple of minutes until cooked through.

Meanwhile wash the spinach. Heat the remaining butter in a pan, drop in the damp spinach and let it cook for 2 or 3 minutes until wilted.

County chef:
Rupert Rowley
Restaurant:
Fischer's Baslow Hall

This restaurant has held a Michelin star since 1994 when owner Max Fischer was chef. He retired from the kitchen in 2002 and handed over to Rupert Rowley, who has maintained the high standards – Baslow Hall was awarded four AA rosettes in 2009.

Rupert loves living and working in the countryside and seeing the animals and fields of fruit and vegetables all around him. He enjoys being able to pick ingredients, such as wild berries and garlic, as he walks to work and have them on the restaurant menu later that day.

"Much of Derbyshire is within the Peak District National Park – a glorious area of dramatic moorland, gentle hills and more rugged landscapes. There are interesting towns in Derbyshire, too, such as the market town of Chesterfield and Buxton, which is a spa town, but the place for us was Matlock, as it's well known as a motorcycle Mecca. On Sundays, the twisty lanes and rolling hills in the area are packed with bikers showing off their skills and their shiny machines.

But on to food. There used to be lots of market gardeners in Derbyshire, but there are far fewer now. We met Barry Hodgkinson, who's aiming to reverse the decline and has created the South Derbyshire Growers' Association to support small growers and help them to market their products. Game is a big thing in Derbyshire and we visited the Calke Estate, which is home to herds of red and fallow deer. They sell their fantastic venison to local farm shops and restaurants and we bought some for our cook-off dish (see page 70)."

Derbyshire

Raspberry Bakewell Pudding

They're good bakers in Derbyshire and feelings run high about Bakewell tart and Bakewell pudding, both traditional dishes. Two shops in Bakewell offer what they say is the original recipe. We tried our hand at a pudding and it went down well.

Serves 6

1 packet of puff pastry
4–5 tbsp seedless raspberry jam
150g fresh raspberries
100g unsalted butter
100g caster sugar
5 eggs
150g ground almonds
a few drops of almond essence
icing sugar and clotted cream to serve

Preheat the oven to 190°C/Gas 5. Roll out the pastry and line a loose-bottomed flan tin with a diameter of 25cm. Leave the excess pastry hanging over the sides and trim once the tart is assembled.

Carefully spread the raspberry jam on the pastry base. Take 3 or 4 spoonfuls of raspberries and crush them lightly, then place them evenly over the jam.

tart and pud:
A Bakewell tart has a shortcrust pastry shell, with a layer of jam, then a spongelike filling that contains ground almonds. There may also be a topping of almonds. The pudding has a puff pastry shell, a layer of jam and then a more custard-like filling.

Cream the butter and sugar in a large bowl until light and fluffy. Gradually add the eggs one at a time, followed by a good spoonful of the ground almonds. Repeat, alternating eggs and almonds until they have all been used up. Add a few drops of almond essence. Pour this mixture into the pastry case and gently spread the mixture evenly with a palette knife. You can trim off the excess pastry now or once cooked – it's up to you. Bake on the middle shelf of the oven for 35–45 minutes until lightly browned on top.

To serve
Dust with icing sugar and serve with the remaining raspberries and a good dollop of clotted cream.

Rupert Rowley's Slow-cooked Derbyshire Lamb

with oatcake crust and wild garlic and rosemary jus

Rupert uses methocel in his mousse. This effectively makes a jelly that is warm and solid on the plate but melts as it cools in the mouth. You can buy it in health food shops or from online culinary suppliers.

Serves 2

Lamb and oatcake crust

1 garlic clove

50g Little Derby cheese

20g thyme

20g chives

20g parsley

1 bay leaf

6 garlic leaves

1 oatcake

1 rack of lamb

30ml olive oil

1 sprig of thyme

1 sprig of rosemary

Caramelised onion mousse

6 onions, finely diced

50g butter

2.5g methocel

75g chicken stock

Wild garlic and rosemary jus

1 carrot

1 onion

1 celery stick

1 dsrtsp tomato purée

½ bottle white wine

bones and trimmings of the rack of lamb

500ml chicken stock

10 wild garlic leaves

1 sprig of rosemary

a new technique:
The sous-vide (water bath) method of cooking is popular in professional kitchens. To do this, you need a precise, temperature-controlled water bath and a vac-pack machine, which most people, us included, don't have. It's interesting to find out about the technique, but if you want to make your own version of this dish, just cook the meat in your usual way.

To prepare the oatcake crust

Peel the garlic and grate the cheese. Pick the leaves off the herbs – vary the amounts depending on which you prefer. Place the herbs, garlic and oatcake in a food processor and blend until you have a paste. Roll this out between 2 sheets of silicone paper and refrigerate until later.

To make the caramelised onion mousse

Cook the onions in the butter in a pan with a lid until they are soft – this should take about an hour – then purée in a liquidiser.

Dissolve the methocel in the chicken stock and fold it into the onion purée. Season the mixture with salt and pepper and pipe into individual moulds. Cook in a water bath at 70°C for 10 minutes.

To prepare the lamb
Remove all the bones and sinew so you are just left with the eye of meat. Lightly season the meat and put into a vacuum bag with 30ml of olive oil and small sprigs of thyme and rosemary. Cook the lamb in a water bath at 57°C for 25 minutes. Remove the meat and sear in a very hot pan until coloured on all sides.

To make the jus

to serve:

Serve some lamb on each plate and add a mousse and some oatcake crust. Drizzle on the jus and serve with a selection of seasonal veg.

Preheat the oven to 180°C/Gas 4 and roast the bones and trimmings until golden brown. Put all the vegetables in a hot pan with the oil on top of the stove and cook until coloured. Add the tomato purée, then deglaze the pan with half a bottle of white wine and reduce by half. Add the bones and trimmings and cover with stock. Add the garlic leaves and rosemary and simmer for 3 hours. Pass through a fine sieve and reduce until you have a sauce consistency.

Loin of Venison
with sloe gin glaze, bubble and squeak and candied shallots

Saddle of venison has very little fat so we wrapped our meat in pancetta to keep it moist, which works really well. The sloe gin went brilliantly with the meat, as did the candied shallots.

Serves 4

Venison and sloe gin glaze

1 saddle of venison, separated
   into 2 loins
1 tbsp olive oil
1 tsp dried thyme
250g pancetta, thinly sliced
1 tbsp vegetable oil
2 tbsp sloe gin
200ml demi-glace (reduced beef stock)
6 juniper berries, crushed
200g blackberries
knob of butter

Candied shallots

12 shallots, peeled
4 tbsp butter
1 tbsp caster sugar
75ml red wine
50ml port
50ml cassis
250ml good beef stock

1 bay leaf
½ tsp dried thyme
zest of ½ lemon

Bubble and squeak

2 tbsp olive oil
1 leek, washed and sliced
750g good potatoes, boiled,
   mashed and left to cool
500g spring cabbage,
   finely shredded and blanched

Vichy carrots

500g carrots, peeled
   and cut into coin-like slices
Vichy or Badoit mineral water
2 tbsp butter
zest of ½ orange
1 tbsp caster sugar
1 tsp sea salt flakes
1 tbsp chopped chervil

tip:
Don't be put off by the demi-glace in this recipe. It is just good beef stock reduced by half until it is really thick and glossy.

To prepare the venison

Preheat the oven to 180°C/Gas 4. Trim the loins of any fat and sinew – the meat must be perfectly clean. Rub the loin with the olive oil, season lightly, rub in the dried thyme and set aside.

Lay the pancetta out on a piece of clingfilm to make a pancetta sheet. Place the loin on to one end of this and roll up so the loin is wrapped in pancetta. The pancetta will add flavour and keep the venison juicy.

Warm the vegetable oil in a frying pan, the sort with a handle you can put into the oven. When it's hot, sear the loin until the pancetta is beginning to turn golden and is sealed. Then place the meat in the oven for 6–8 minutes. Don't let it overcook, as you want the venison to be pink. Remove the meat from the pan and set aside somewhere warm to rest.

To make the sloe gin glaze

Deglaze the pan with sloe gin and burn off the alcohol. Pour in the demi-glace and add the crushed juniper berries. Simmer for about 5 minutes to reduce the stock and infuse the juniper flavour. Strain the sauce to remove the solids and the crushed berries and discard them. Return the sauce to the pan, add the blackberries and cook for about 4 minutes until the blackberries are softened. Crush slightly, then season with sea salt and black pepper and add the knob of butter to give the sauce a sheen.

To prepare the candied shallots

Carefully simmer the shallots in a pan of boiling water for 5 minutes to soften them up a bit. Melt the butter in a frying pan, add the shallots and cook until brown. Add the sugar and stir until the butter starts to caramelise. Mix the wine, port, cassis and stock together. Add about a quarter of this mixture to the pan, bring to the boil and add the bay leaf, thyme and lemon zest. Keep adding the remaining liquid and cook it down until the shallots are sticky and glazed. Set them aside until ready to serve.

to serve:

Cut the loin into thick slices, allowing about three per portion. Top with the glaze and add the bubble and squeak and candied shallots. Pipe on some blobs of carrot and garnish with chopped chervil. Good served with some broccoli and roasted tomatoes.

To make the bubble and squeak

Heat a little of the oil in a frying pan and sweat the leek until cooked. Mix the leek with the potato and cabbage and season to taste. Add the rest of the oil to the frying pan. Place the 4 chef's rings into this pan and pack with bubble and squeak. Leave until the vegetables are crispy and cooked through and turn when they are golden on the bottom.

To prepare the Vichy carrots

Put the carrot slices into a saucepan. Add the mineral water to just cover the carrots, then add the butter, orange zest, sugar and salt. Simmer for about 15 minutes until the water has been absorbed and the carrots are cooked through. Add the chervil and black pepper to taste. Process to a fine purée, then transfer and reheat. Spoon into a piping bag.

County chef:
Will Furlong
Restaurant:
Auchen Castle

An 18th-century castle transformed into a luxury hotel, Auchen Castle is set in breathtaking countryside. Its restaurant is run by Will Furlong who has worked as a chef for 32 years, nearly all of those in Scotland. He describes his cooking as 'Scottish with a twist' and says that Dumfries and Galloway has the best produce in all of Scotland. In particular, he believes that the game, beef and salmon are of the highest quality you can find anywhere in the world. Will is passionate about cooking and confesses that his wife claims he is married to his kitchen, not to her!

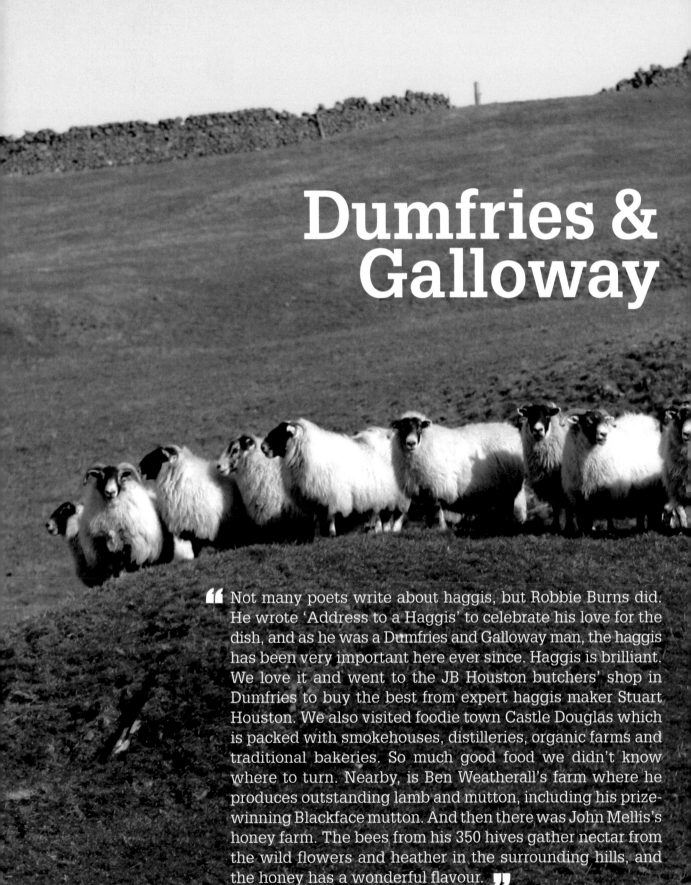

Dumfries & Galloway

" Not many poets write about haggis, but Robbie Burns did. He wrote 'Address to a Haggis' to celebrate his love for the dish, and as he was a Dumfries and Galloway man, the haggis has been very important here ever since. Haggis is brilliant. We love it and went to the JB Houston butchers' shop in Dumfries to buy the best from expert haggis maker Stuart Houston. We also visited foodie town Castle Douglas which is packed with smokehouses, distilleries, organic farms and traditional bakeries. So much good food we didn't know where to turn. Nearby, is Ben Weatherall's farm where he produces outstanding lamb and mutton, including his prize-winning Blackface mutton. And then there was John Mellis's honey farm. The bees from his 350 hives gather nectar from the wild flowers and heather in the surrounding hills, and the honey has a wonderful flavour. "

Clapshot, Haggis and Whisky Sauce

Haggis with a touch of whisky – what could be better? Haggis used to be a bit of a faff to cook, but it's much easier now with aluminium foil. Just wrap it up neatly and bake in the oven – the haggis cooks in its own juices. Simple!

Serves 4

500g haggis

500g floury potatoes

500g turnips

50g butter

75ml double cream

sea salt

freshly ground white pepper

2 tbsp chopped chives

500ml double cream

2 tsp grain mustard

1 tbsp Dijon mustard

2 tsp whisky

juice of ½ lemon

Preheat the oven to 180°C/Gas 4. Wrap the haggis tightly in aluminium foil and bake for 45 minutes.

Peel the potatoes and turnips, and cut them into equal-sized pieces. Cook in separate pans of boiling, salted water until tender. Mash them together and add the butter, 75ml of cream and seasoning. Stir in half the chopped chives and keep warm while you make the sauce.

more about haggis:
People get a bit squeamish about the ingredients in haggis. Basically it's made of heart, liver and lungs and each adds its own texture and culinary qualities to the dish. Good haggis contains good-quality ingredients so don't worry.

Gently heat the 500ml of cream in a saucepan and add the mustards and the whisky. Turn the heat up high to cook out the alcohol. Season to taste and add the remaining chives. Just before serving, whisk in the lemon juice.

To serve

Put a good spoonful of mash (clapshot) on a warm plate. Top with some haggis and drizzle over the warm whisky sauce.

Will Furlong's Fillet of Buccleuch Beef

with haggis-stuffed tomato, savoy cabbage, potato rosti and Auchen Castle whisky jus

Buccleuch beef comes from grass-fed cattle reared in Dumfries and is some of the best you can get.

Serves 4

Fillet steaks
olive oil
4 x 225g fillets of Buccleuch beef

Whisky jus
1kg oxtail bones
1 onion, roughly chopped
4 carrots, roughly chopped
250g tomato purée
100g redcurrant jelly
250ml double cream
50ml whisky

Potato rosti
3 baking potatoes, peeled
1 large red onion, peeled
3 egg yolks

Haggis-stuffed tomatoes
4 tomatoes
250g haggis

Savoy cabbage
1 large savoy cabbage
200g salted butter

To make the whisky jus
Roast the oxtail bones in a hot oven until brown. Put them in a large pan with 4 litres of water and add the onion, carrots and tomato purée. Boil for about 2–3 hours or until the stock has reduced to about 1 litre.

Remove the bones, add the redcurrant jelly and bring the stock back to the boil. Then add 250ml of double cream and reduce for a further 15 minutes until the sauce is thick and shiny. Remove from the heat, and keep warm.

To cook the fillet steaks
Preheat the oven to 160°C/Gas 3. Heat a pan and add some olive oil and seal the fillets for 1 minute on each side. Put the steaks on to a baking tray (saving the oil in the pan for later) and cook in the preheated oven for 20 minutes. Check the meat and if it is too rare for your taste, cook for another 5 minutes. Allow to rest before serving.

tip:

A good tip Will showed us was a way of keeping a sauce warm. Just pour the sauce into a jam jar, put the lid on and set it in a pan of hot water. When you're ready to serve, take it out carefully with a cloth and give it a good shake. This way it doesn't form a skin.

To make the potato rosti

Using a mandolin, slice the potatoes into fine strips. Slice the onion in the same way. Mix the potato and onion together in a bowl, add salt and pepper and bind with the egg yolks. Divide the mixture between 4 chef's rings and seal in a hot pan, using the same oil as used to seal the beef. Brown on both sides and then place the rosti portions on a baking sheet and cook in the preheated oven (160°C/Gas 3) for 20 minutes.

to serve:

Slice the fillets at an angle. Reheat the cabbage and pile it in the centre of the plate, with some slices of beef on top. Take a potato rosti out of its ring and put it on the corner of the plate. Add a tomato and the jus on

To prepare the haggis-stuffed tomatoes

Cut the tops off the tomatoes and take a small slice off the bottom so that the tomatoes stand upright. Using a spoon, carefully remove the insides. Divide the haggis into 4 pieces and shape into small balls. Put 1 haggis ball inside each tomato and cook the stuffed tomatoes for 20 minutes – again at 160°C/Gas 3.

To prepare the savoy cabbage

Shred the cabbage, taking care to remove the core. Wash the cabbage in cold water – this

Mutton and Caper Pudding
with honey-glazed baby vegetables and fondant potatoes

You will need four small basins, buttered and floured, for the puddings. It's worth sourcing mutton for this – it really does have a great flavour.

Serves 4

Filling

500g shoulder of mutton
2 tbsp plain flour
1 onion and 1 carrot, finely chopped
1 leek, finely chopped
½ celery stick, finely chopped
1 garlic clove, finely crushed
100ml Madeira, plus extra for gravy
500ml beef stock
10 anchovy fillets, finely chopped
2 tbsp capers, finely chopped
2 tbsp chopped parsley

Suet case

375g self-raising flour
200g beef suet
1 tsp dried rosemary
½ tsp dried sage

1 tsp sea salt
1 egg yolk and 1 beaten egg

Fondant potatoes

4 potatoes
150g butter
1 garlic clove
75ml chicken stock

Honey-glazed baby vegetables

50g butter
1 tbsp caraway seeds
1 tbsp thyme
250g each of baby carrots, baby leeks
 and baby beetroot, trimmed and blanched
salt and freshly ground white pepper
100m runny honey
1 tsp balsamic vinegar

To make the mutton and caper pudding

First make the filling. Trim the mutton and cut into 1cm cubes, saving the fat and trimmings. Render down the fat and trimmings in a casserole dish, discarding any large pieces.

Roll the mutton cubes in the flour and fry them in the rendered fat until brown. Remove the mutton and set aside, then sweat the onion, carrot, leek and celery in the same fat for about 5 minutes. Add the garlic and sweat for another minute. Return the meat to the pan and add the Madeira and stock. Season with a little pepper, cover the dish and braise gently for 2–2½ hours at about 170°C/Gas 3 until the meat is tender. Leave to cool. Once cooled, add the chopped anchovies, capers and parsley and check the seasoning.

tip:

It's always best to use dried herbs in a suet crust. They come to life and give more flavour as they rehydrate. Fresh herbs just go soggy as the crust cooks.

Now make the suet case. Mix the flour, suet, rosemary, sage and salt in a bowl. Then slowly add some water at room temperature until a firm dough is formed. Knead in the egg yolk and put the dough in the fridge to chill for about an hour.

Take a ball of dough and roll it out thinly into a round shape. Using the end of a rolling pin, fold the dough over the edges to make a cup shape. Place a buttered and floured pudding basin on top and then turn it upright and remove the rolling pin. This will ensure that the crust lines the basin properly. Fill the suet case with meat and top up with a little of the cooking liquid to keep the meat moist. Roll out a smaller ball to make the lid, place it on top and brush with a little beaten egg around the edges. Use a rolling pin to roll around the edge to trim and seal the top to the sides. Double-wrap tightly with foil. Repeat to make the other 3 puddings. Steam them for about 30 minutes in a covered pan of boiling water or in a steamer.

another tip:

Trimming the edges of the potatoes for the fondant isn't just for show. It makes them easier to turn and stops them sticking to the pan.

To make the gravy

Pass the remaining contents of the casserole dish through a sieve and strain the liquid from the cooking juices into a saucepan. Add a little Madeira and return to the heat to burn off the alcohol. Keep warm until ready to serve.

To make the fondant potatoes

Peel the potatoes and trim off the tops and bottoms so they are flat. With a pastry cutter, cut the potatoes into round shapes to make perfect cylinders about 2cm high. Using a potato peeler, neatly cut around the top edge at an angle of 45 degrees to make bevelled edges. Melt the butter in a medium pan and add the crushed garlic and potato rounds. Cook until the potatoes are golden brown on the bottom, taking care not to let the butter burn. Once golden, turn the potatoes over, add the stock and season well. Cover with greaseproof paper and simmer gently until the potatoes are cooked through.

to serve:

Remove the puddings from their basins and place one on each plate – drizzle with a little extra sauce if necessary. Place a fondant potato and some honey-glazed baby vegetables either side and drizzle on the sauce to finish.

To prepare the honey-glazed baby vegetables

Heat the butter in a pan until it foams. Add the caraway seeds, thyme and blanched vegetables. Season with salt and freshly ground white pepper, then add the honey. Cook until all the vegetables are al dente and the honey has thickened. Just before serving, drizzle over a little balsamic vinegar.

County chef:
Mark Baumann
Restaurant:
Baumann's Brasserie

Mark Baumann runs Baumann's Brasserie in the market town of Coggeshall. He set up the restaurant in 1986 with his business partner, the late Peter Langan, and it has been thriving ever since. Mark prides himself on his seasonal menu and he is passionate about local produce. He even had his own television series called *Baumann Goes to Market*, which focused on locally produced, British food, and he wants to promote Essex as a foodie destination.

"Our trip down to Essex on the bikes was probably the worst ever – and we've ridden across the Namibian desert! It was just after the snow so the weather was bitterly cold and the roads were in a terrible state. We were glad to get there, we can tell you. Because Essex is so close to London we were surprised at how strong its personality is as a county. People are really proud of their heritage and local dishes, and we met people whose families had lived in Essex for generations. We found wonderful seafood, such as oysters and cockles; lots of local food producers, and learned about the importance of saffron and sea salt in the county.

Some of the highlights of the trip were meeting Paul Kelly, turkey rearer, and visiting the Tiptree jam people. Paul really cares about his birds. They are free-range, eat good food and live a decent life, so they taste great. The Wilkin family have been growing and preserving fruit at Tiptree for almost 150 years and they still use proper fruit, not purée like most companies. We loved their crab apple jelly. "

Essex

Oysters Mornay

Buy the best-quality, freshest oysters you can find. If any of the oysters are dry inside when they are shucked, discard them. When shucking oysters, use a thick tea towel to hold the oyster and open them from the narrow end of the shell using a short-bladed knife.

Serves 4–6

Oysters mornay

60g unsalted butter

2 tbsp plain flour

500ml whole milk

110g strong Cheddar cheese, grated

24 oysters, shucked and turned
    presentation side up in the shell

2 tbsp curly parsley, finely chopped

Traditional oysters

as many oysters as you can eat (native or rock)

bag of ice

3 tbsp red wine vinegar

5 tbsp finely chopped shallots

Tabasco sauce

Worcestershire sauce

1 lemon, cut into wedges

To make the oysters mornay

Get your grill really hot. Melt the butter in a saucepan, add the flour and cook for a few minutes. Add the milk and stir to make a thick white sauce. Stir in half the cheese and check the seasoning. Place the oysters in rows in a grill pan, add a spoonful of cheese sauce on to each oyster and sprinkle the remaining cheese on top. Grill until golden and scatter with parsley before serving.

To prepare traditional oysters

Shuck the oysters, keeping all the juices inside, and put them on a plate of ice. Whisk the vinegar with the shallots in a ramekin and set aside for 5 minutes to infuse. Pile crushed ice on to a large serving dish. This will hold the oysters steady and also keep them cool. Arrange the oysters on the ice and serve with the red wine vinegar and shallots, Tabasco and Worcestershire sauce and lemon wedges.

Cockle Chowder

We ate delicious cockles in Southend – sprinkled with malt vinegar and white pepper and eaten out of a paper bag – but we also made this great chowder.

Serves 4–6

25g unsalted butter

1 tbsp olive oil

4 rashers of streaky bacon, shredded

1 large onion, finely diced

400g cooked shelled cockles
  or 1kg raw cockles in the shell

250ml dry white wine

3 floury potatoes, peeled and cubed

500ml milk

2 tbsp chopped curly parsley

1 tbsp chopped fresh thyme

2 tbsp double cream

In a big saucepan, heat the butter and the olive oil, add the bacon and cook until coloured. Add the onion and sweat until transparent – this will take about 5 minutes.

If using raw cockles, wash them well or place them in a bowl of water, with some bran or porridge oats for a few hours and they will clean themselves inside and out. Whatever you do, make sure they are thoroughly clean. Add the wine to the saucepan with the bacon and onion and bring to a rolling boil. Pour in the cockles and boil for a few minutes. They are done when the shells open. Lift out the cockles with a slotted spoon and set them aside to cool, keeping the cooking liquor. Pick the cockles from the shells, discarding any that have not opened. If you're using ready-cooked cockles, simply add the wine to the pan and reduce by half.

Meanwhile, in a separate saucepan, par-boil the potatoes for about 5 minutes until just soft. Drain and set aside. Place the cockle and bacon juices in a pan, bring to a simmer, then add the milk and the potatoes. Simmer until the potatoes just start to disintegrate. Add the cockles, parsley, thyme and cream. Cook for a couple of minutes, but be careful not to overcook the cockles. Season to taste with sea salt flakes and ground white pepper and serve with a hunk of sourdough bread and butter.

Mark Baumann's
Rolled Loin of Lamb
with lobster and basil mousse, cheesy mustard mash and lamb jus

This is a superb dish. Like many chefs, Mark uses pig's caul to keep the meat moist as it cooks. Caul is the stomach lining of a pig, sheep or cow, and your butcher should be able to supply it.

Serves 4

Basil purée
4 bunches of basil, leaves only

Lobster and basil mousse
1 carrot and 1 small onion, peeled
1 celery stick
1 bay leaf
1 bunch of tarragon
6 peppercorns
Maldon sea salt
1 litre water
110ml white wine
1 live lobster, about 500g in weight
200g chicken breast
200g fresh salmon fillet
2 egg whites
50ml double cream

Cheesy mustard mash
1kg floury potatoes, such as Maris Piper
110g cheddar cheese, grated
50g grain mustard

1 bunch of parsley, finely chopped
1 bunch of chives, finely chopped

Rolled loin of lamb
110g baby spinach leaves, washed
1 boned loin of lamb
 with fat left on and rind removed
200g caul (pig's stomach lining)
olive oil
1 handful of fresh rosemary

Asparagus and baby vegetables
150g each of asparagus, baby carrots,
 baby leeks and baby turnips
400g unsalted butter
400ml vegetable stock
50g sugar

Lamb jus
50ml red wine
cooking juices from the loin of lamb
25g unsalted butter

To make the basil purée
Put the basil leaves into boiling salted water and cook for 30 seconds. Strain and plunge into cold water to refresh. When the blanched basil is cold, drain and squeeze out any excess water. Put the basil into a blender and blitz to make a smooth purée. You may need to add a couple of drops of water to get the right consistency.

To make the lobster and basil mousse

Chop the vegetables and place them in a pan with the bay leaf, tarragon, peppercorns and a little sea salt. Add the water and white wine and bring to the boil. When the stock has boiled, place the live lobster into the pan and cook for 8 minutes. Refresh the lobster in a bowl of ice-cold water and leave to cool. Take the lobster meat out of the shell and neatly dice into 1cm pieces. Blitz the chicken breast and salmon fillet in a blender. When the mixture is smooth, add the egg whites a little at a time, followed by the double cream. Transfer to a cold bowl, season to taste and add the basil purée to turn the mousse bright green. Fold the diced lobster meat into the mousse.

tip:
Be brave with the mustard in this mash recipe. It really does taste good.

To make the cheesy mustard mash

Peel the potatoes and cut them into equal-sized pieces. Fill a saucepan with water and bring to the boil. Reduce the heat and add the potatoes with a generous sprinkling of salt. Try not to boil the water, letting the potatoes stew instead. When the potatoes are cooked, drain them and return to a low heat to remove any excess moisture. Mash the potatoes and add the cheese and grain mustard. Before serving, add the herbs and mix well.

To prepare the rolled loin of lamb

Preheat the oven to 180°C/Gas 4. Blanch the spinach in boiling salted water for 10 seconds and refresh in ice-cold water. Take the spinach out and pat dry. Trim any excess fat from the lamb, but make sure you keep the 'skirt' of fat running from the loin. Using a rolling pin or meat tenderiser, beat the skirt of fat to make a thin flap extending out from the loin. Place the blanched spinach leaves on to the thinned fat and spread the lobster mousse over the top. Season the loin with sea salt and black pepper and roll it up tightly, taking care not to let the mousse escape. Roll several layers of caul around the loin and tie with butcher's string to secure it. Leave to chill for about an hour in the fridge.

to serve:
Add the herbs to the mash and spoon mash and lobster mousse on to each plate. Carve the loin into 1–2cm slices and add 2 to each serving. Neatly arrange the asparagus and baby vegetables around the lamb and spoon the jus over and around.

Heat a heavy-based pan and add a little oil. Roll the loin in the pan on all sides until it is golden brown, then place in the oven. After 10 minutes, take the pan out, lift the lamb and put a handful of fresh rosemary in the bottom of the pan. Sit the loin back on top of the rosemary and roast for a further few minutes. Take the lamb out of the oven and pour the cooking juices into a saucepan. Leave the loin to rest.

To prepare the asparagus and baby vegetables

In separate pans, blanch the asparagus in boiling water for 30 seconds and all the other vegetables for 1 minute. Drain the water and add butter, vegetable stock and sugar to each pan and return to the heat. Leave to cook gently until al dente. Season with salt and black pepper.

To make the lamb jus

Add the red wine to the lamb cooking juices. Reduce for a few minutes and add the butter.

Stuffed Turkey Ballotine
with garlic and saffron mashed potatoes, crab apple jelly gravy and roasted green beans

Paul Kelly's birds are known as the 'Rolls Royce' of turkeys and have the best texture and flavour. Just be careful not to overcook your turkey.

Serves 4–6

Turkey ballotine

12 rashers streaky bacon, skin removed and stretched flat

1.5kg large turkey breast crown, boned but skin intact

400g minced veal shoulder

1 chicken liver, chopped

30g unsalted butter

1 level tbsp cornflour

150ml milk

2 egg whites, lightly beaten

30g shelled pistachios, halved

1 small green pepper, seeded and diced

½ tsp ground nutmeg

3 sage leaves, chopped

½ tsp sea salt flakes

½ tsp ground white pepper

olive oil

Garlic saffron mashed potatoes

1kg potatoes, peeled and quartered

75ml single cream

1 pinch saffron, crushed

50g unsalted butter

3 garlic cloves, crushed

Crab apple jelly gravy

juices from the turkey ballotine

1 tbsp Tiptree crab apple jelly

25g butter

Roasted green beans

2 tbsp extra virgin olive oil

zest of 1 large lemon,

1 tsp chopped fresh rosemary

1 tsp fresh thyme

500g fine green beans

To prepare the turkey ballotine

Preheat the oven to 150°C/Gas 2. Place the turkey on a work surface, split open the thick part of the breast and butterfly it outwards to make a roughly rectangular shape. Cover the turkey with clingfilm and beat it flat with a rolling pin. Lay the bacon in strips on a sheet of clingfilm with the edges overlapping slightly to make a continuous 'blanket'. This is to keep the turkey juicy while cooking as well as for decoration. Place the turkey skin-side down on one end of the bacon, with the clingfilm still underneath the bacon.

Next, make the stuffing. Put the veal in a food processor. Add the chicken liver and process until very smooth, then turn it into a bowl. Melt the butter in a saucepan, stir in the cornflour and add the milk. Cook until it thickens. Leave to cool for 5 minutes, then stir into the minced veal and chicken liver. Fold in the egg whites, pistachios, green pepper, nutmeg, sage and seasoning.

Peel the clingfilm off the top of the turkey and spread the stuffing in a line along the long edge. Roll over tightly, using the clingfilm under the bacon to help you make a neat sausage shape. Remove the clingfilm and then roll the whole lot in a couple of layers of aluminium foil, making sure the roll is as tight as possible. Put a tablespoon of olive oil in a roasting tin, add the ballotine, cover with more foil, and roast for 1½–2 hours. At the end of the cooking time, remove the foil and pour off any juices from the roasting tin into a saucepan. Heat the grill and place the turkey under the grill to brown, turning regularly for even colouring. Set aside to rest.

To make the garlic saffron mashed potatoes

Put the potatoes into a pan of salted water, bring to the boil and simmer for about 20 minutes until they are soft. Meanwhile, warm the cream in a pan with the saffron and leave to infuse.

Melt the butter in a separate pan and add the crushed garlic. Warm very slowly without browning to soften the garlic and infuse the butter. Drain the potatoes and return to the pan to drive off any excess moisture, then mash. Mix in the saffron cream and the garlic butter and season to taste.

To make the crab apple jelly gravy

Reduce the cooking juices from the turkey ballotine until they are rich and thickened. Stir in the crab apple jelly and add the butter.

To prepare the roasted beans

Preheat the oven to 200°C/Gas 6. Warm the oil in a pan, add the lemon zest and let it sizzle gently for about 30 seconds. Leave to cool for a couple of minutes, then stir in the herbs and leave to infuse for 20 minutes. Put the beans in a bowl and pour in the oil. Make sure the beans are well covered with oil, then season liberally with sea salt and ground black pepper. Put the beans on a baking tray and roast in the oven for 10–15 minutes until they are tender and starting to colour. Serve with a squeeze of lemon if you fancy – the sharpness of the beans will work well with the crab apple jelly.

To serve

Carve the turkey into generous slices. Pipe some mash on to the centre of each plate and top with a slice of the turkey ballotine. Scatter the beans around the edge of the plate, then spoon over the gravy.

County chef:
Noel McMeel
Restaurant:
Catalina at the Lough Erne Golf Resort

Noel McMeel is the head chef at the Catalina Restaurant at the Lough Erne Golf Resort, a five-star hotel and spa on the banks of Lough Erne. Noel grew up on a farm in County Antrim and developed a love of food at an early age. He has cooked at top restaurants in the United States, but his dream was always to come back to Northern Ireland. He has won acclaim for his modern approach to Irish cooking and is passionate about finding, as he says, fresh local ingredients that explode with flavour.

Fermanagh

"We had such a warm welcome in this breathtakingly beautiful county. People were so hospitable, it was amazing – we're still recovering. Fermanagh is steeped in food traditions and the locals love cooking. We found the best bacon in the world here when we went to Pat O'Doherty's shop in Enniskillen and tried his famous Black Bacon — never tasted anything like it. Pat's pigs live on an island he bought in Upper Lough Erne and they can roam freely, root around and live with very little interference. Heaven for pigs.

We relish any opportunity to go fishing so it was a real treat to go fly-fishing for brown trout with Patrick Trotter in Lough Erne. Brown trout are an indigenous species and the waters here suit them well so they thrive. We had a great day and caught some trout to use in our stuffed brown trout dish (see page 94). "

Boxty
with crispy bacon and maple syrup

Boxty is a traditional Northern Irish dish made with cooked mashed potatoes and raw potatoes. Some excellent dry-cured bacon is just the thing with this.

Serves 4–6

500g raw potatoes, grated
500g cold mashed potatoes
1 heaped tsp baking powder
3 cups plain flour
large knob of butter, melted
about 200ml milk
olive oil
8–12 smoked bacon rashers
maple syrup, to drizzle

Squeeze the grated raw potatoes in a tea towel to get rid of any liquid, then mix the raw potato with the mashed potatoes. In a separate bowl, stir the baking powder into the flour. Add this to the potatoes and mix well. Stir in the melted butter and season with salt and pepper. Beat in the milk, adding a little extra if necessary to make a heavy batter. Set aside.

Heat a touch of oil in a large non-stick frying pan and cook the bacon rashers until crisp and golden on both sides. Remove the bacon from the pan and set aside.

Spoon blobs of the boxty mixture into the hot oil and bacon juices. Fry for a few minutes on each side until golden brown and cooked through.

To serve
Serve the boxty with some crispy bacon alongside it and drizzle with maple syrup.

local lore:
There's a local rhyme about boxty:
'Boxty on the griddle
Boxty on the pan
If you canna make boxty
You'll never get your man.'

Noel McMeel's Lough Erne Mixed Grill

You'll need to plan ahead for this one as the confit of belly pork is best prepared a week in advance for maximum flavour.

Serves 4

Confit of belly pork
2 sprigs of rosemary, chopped
4 bay leaves
1 tsp ground black pepper
2 tsp salt
500g sugar
olive oil
2kg belly pork
2 litres of melted duck fat

Lamb cutlets
8 lamb cutlets, trimmed of fat
1½ lemons
50ml extra virgin olive oil
1 large garlic clove, chopped finely
1 bunch of flat-leaf parsley, chopped finely
1 tsp finely chopped fresh rosemary

Fillet steak (Kettyle Irish beef)
8 x 100–150g fillet steaks (centre cut)
50ml sunflower oil

Seared lambs' kidneys
8 baby vine tomatoes
3 tbsp olive oil
1 garlic clove
3 tbsp butter
1 tbsp vegetable oil
400g lambs' kidneys
4 tbsp finely minced onion
1 cup cleaned and sliced mushrooms
60ml red wine

Béarnaise sauce
2 egg yolks
1 tbsp lemon juice
100ml clarified butter
pinch of cayenne pepper or hot paprika
¼ tsp salt
1 tbsp chopped tarragon

Chunky chips
16 large floury potatoes
500ml vegetable oil

Poached eggs and spinach
8 large free-range eggs
50ml vinegar
1 handful of fresh spinach leaves
butter

to serve:
Place a fillet steak at one end of a rectangular plate with some kidney and baby tomatoes on top. Add a lamb cutlet next to the steak and some cooked belly pork. Place four chunky chips on top of each other with the fresh sautéed spinach under the freshly poached egg. Spoon a tablespoon of béarnaise sauce over the poached egg and serve.

To prepare the confit of belly pork
Mix the rosemary, bay leaves, pepper, salt and sugar with some olive oil to make a paste. Rub into the pork and leave to marinate overnight. Next day, rinse the pork twice and then submerge it in the duck fat. Place on a baking tray and cook in a low oven, 120°C/Gas ½ for 3 hours. Leave the pork to cool in the fat, then store for a week in the fridge to allow the tasty flavours to develop fully. When ready to serve, divide the pork into 8 pieces and pan-fry to warm through and crisp the skin.

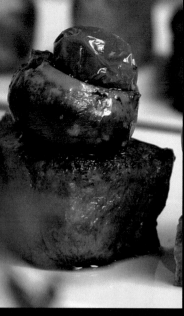

To prepare the lamb cutlets

Find a dish that will hold all the cutlets laid flat. Mix together the juice of 1 lemon with the oil, garlic and herbs and rub on to the lamb. Once they are all well covered, leave to marinate for at least half an hour.

Heat a pan until searingly hot. Liberally sprinkle the cutlets with salt on both sides and add pepper to taste. Place the cutlets flat in the pan. Once the meat is seared on both sides, reduce the heat and add any leftover marinade. Squeeze the juice of the other half of lemon on to the cutlets and cook for a further 6 minutes – the meat should be pink in the middle. Rest for 1–2 minutes before serving.

To prepare the fillet steaks

Take the fillet steaks out of the fridge at least 20 minutes before cooking to allow them to reach room temperature. Pat the steaks with kitchen paper to remove any excess moisture. Rub a little sunflower oil into the steaks with your fingers (don't use olive oil as it burns at too low a temperature), and leave to sit for a few minutes. Season with salt and pepper if you like. Put a frying pan on the biggest ring or burner on your hob. When the pan is as hot as you can get it, gently add the steaks. After 30 seconds or so, move them so that they don't stick and burn. The exact cooking time depends on how hot your pan is and the size of the steak, but 2–3 minutes each side should give nice medium-rare meat.

To prepare the seared lambs' kidneys

Submerge the tomatoes in olive oil and garlic and leave at room temperature for up to 2 hours. Remove the outside membrane from the kidneys (you can ask your butcher to do this for you), rinse them well, pat dry and set aside. Melt the butter and vegetable oil together in a frying pan. Brown the kidneys quickly, gently turning them, and then put them on a warm platter. Add the onion and mushrooms to the pan and cook until the onion is soft and translucent, stirring frequently. Add the wine and cook for another minute or so. Return the kidneys to the pan and add salt to taste. Heat through for a few minutes. Cut the kidneys in half lengthways before serving.

To make the béarnaise sauce

Bring a pan of water to the boil, then turn it down to a simmer. Place a heatproof bowl over the pan, making sure the base is not touching the water. Add the egg yolks and lemon juice and whisk until the mixture doubles in volume (the eggs need to cook slightly without turning into scrambled eggs). Add the butter and keep stirring, making sure that the water underneath does not boil as it will curdle the eggs. Keep stirring, until the sauce thickens – this can take a while. Add the cayenne pepper or hot paprika, salt and tarragon.

To make the chunky chips

Peel the potatoes and cut them into pieces measuring about 1cm thick x 7–8cm long. Discard any trimmings. Wash the chips to get rid of the excess starch and pat them dry. Heat the oil to 150°C in a deep-fat fryer. Put in a chip to test the heat – it should rise slowly to the surface covered in small bubbles. Cook the chips a handful at a time, allowing 6–7 minutes for each batch. When all the chips are cooked, raise the temperature of the oil to 180°C and put all the chips back in the pan for another 4–5 minutes until golden. Drain on absorbent paper and sprinkle with fine salt before serving.

To poach the eggs and cook the spinach

Poach the eggs, adding a little vinegar to the water. Remove and drain on kitchen paper. Briefly cook the spinach in the butter in a warm pan until wilted, then drain and season.

Stuffed Brown Trout
with rhubarb compote and watercress quenelle

The rhubarb compote goes beautifully with this trout or with other fish, such as grilled sea bass. Like lemon, rhubarb adds a touch of sharpness, which sets off the flavour of the fish.

Serves 4

Baked stuffed trout
4 wild brown trout, gutted
12 x 25g knobs of butter
fresh herbs, such as parsley,
   chives and tarragon
white wine
olive oil

Watercress quenelle
200g watercress

1 Chinese cabbage, shredded
50g pine nuts
2 tbsp extra virgin olive oil
2 tsp lemon juice
chicken stock

Rhubarb compote
6 sticks of rhubarb, roughly chopped
50–60g soft brown sugar
1 star anise

To prepare the baked stuffed trout
Preheat the oven to 170°C/Gas 3. Cut the heads and tails off the trout (you can ask your fishmonger to do this for you). Slash each side 3 times at an angle, cutting about 0.5cm deep. This stops the fish from curling up while cooking and allows the flavours of the stuffing to permeate the fish. Season inside and out and pack the stomach cavity of each fish with 3 knobs of butter and a handful of herbs. Place each fish on a piece of foil and pour over a splash of white wine and a drizzle of olive oil. Wrap them up, place on a baking tray and put in the oven for 10–15 minutes or until cooked. Serve with a few sea salt crystals on the top.

To make the watercress quenelle
Bring a pan of salted boiling water to the boil and blanch the watercress and Chinese cabbage for 2–3 minutes. Drain and place in a food processor with the pine nuts and olive oil. Blitz until loosened. Add the lemon juice, seasoning and a touch of chicken stock and blitz again until textured but not puréed. Check the seasoning, then transfer to a pan and heat gently.

to serve:
Arrange a baked trout on each plate, with some rhubarb compote and watercress quenelle alongside it.

To make the rhubarb compote
Put the chopped rhubarb, sugar and star anise in a pan, and add a splash of water. Cook for 10–12 minutes over a gentle heat or until the rhubarb has cooked down to a soft purée. Remove the star anise before serving.

County chef:
James Graham
Restaurant:
Allium

Allium, in the pretty town of Fairford, opened in 2004 and has quickly made a name for itself. It has been Michelin listed and won Southwest Restaurant of the Year in 2008.

Owner and head chef James previously worked with Raymond Blanc and describes himself as a 'gutsy chef who is unafraid of flavour'. He loves to use local produce in his varied menus and in the dishes sold in his nearby deli.

He shoots his own venison and works with a local farm to rear poultry to his own specifications.

Gloucestershire

" When you think of Gloucestershire, the rolling countryside and pretty villages are what first come to mind. But we went to cook on Gloucester docks and learned that this was once a major trade port, linked to the Severn Estuary by the network of inland canals. It's a fascinating area and we're happy to say that our squab pie went down well with the locals. Rapeseed oil is becoming increasingly popular and we met the Campbell family who produce some of the best under the name of R-Oil. It has a great colour and flavour, is low in saturated fats and can be used at high temperatures, so is ideal for frying. Good stuff, we thought. We also visited Leonie, who a few years back decided to change her life and start a business rearing top-quality guinea fowl. From the start she worked with local restaurants and chefs to develop the products they wanted while maintaining her ethical standards and keeping her birds in a natural environment. We bought some for our cook-off dish and they were excellent. Also had a great day out at Stroud Farmers' Market – full of local produce and well worth a look. "

Gloucestershire Squab Pie

A squab is a young pigeon, but this traditional pie is actually made with lamb and apples. You will need a large, 2-litre pie dish and a pie funnel.

Serves 6

Filling

3 tbsp plain flour
½ tsp flaked sea salt, plus extra to taste
black pepper
1kg Gloucestershire lamb neck fillet,
    trimmed of excess fat and cut into
    roughly 3cm chunks
2–3 tbsp rapeseed oil
2 medium onions, halved and sliced
½ tsp freshly grated nutmeg
¼ tsp ground allspice
1 sprig of fresh rosemary, leaves
    finely chopped
500ml good fresh chicken or lamb stock

1 medium Bramley apple, peeled,
    quartered, cored and sliced
2 crisp eating apples, peeled,
    quartered, cored and sliced
4 or 5 large fresh sage leaves,
    finely shredded

Pastry

75g lard, cut into small pieces
75g butter, cut into small pieces
300g plain flour, sifted
good pinch of salt
1 medium free-range egg
1 tbsp cold water

To cook the filling

Tip the 3 tablespoons of flour into a large bowl and add the salt and a good grinding of black pepper. Add the lamb and toss well until the meat is lightly coated with a dusting of the seasoned flour. Heat a large non-stick frying pan, add 2 tablespoons of rapeseed oil and cook the lamb chunks in 2 batches, turning every now and then until golden brown on all sides. As the lamb browns, transfer it to a large, heavy-based saucepan or flameproof casserole dish with tongs or a slotted spoon.

Add the onions to the frying pan and cook them in the remaining fat until nicely browned, stirring regularly. Add a little extra oil if the pan seems too dry. Tip the onions into the casserole dish with the lamb and add the nutmeg, allspice and rosemary. Pour in the stock and add an extra 300ml of cold water. Bring the liquid to the boil, then reduce the heat and leave to simmer for 40 minutes or until the lamb is just tender and the liquid has reduced to a good gravy consistency. Season to taste, then remove the pan from the heat, cover and leave to cool for 30 minutes.

To make the pastry

Rub the fats into the flour and salt in a large bowl until the mixture resembles fine breadcrumbs – use a food processor for this if you like.

Beat the egg lightly with the water and put 2 tablespoons of the mixture into a separate bowl to use for the pastry glaze. Make a well in the centre of the flour and add the rest of the egg mixture. Stir with a wooden spoon until the dough comes together, then form into a ball and transfer to a floured surface. Lightly knead the dough, flatten slightly into a round shape and wrap in clingfilm. Chill in the fridge for 30 minutes.

To put the pie together

Once the pie filling has cooled to room temperature, preheat the oven to 200°C/Gas 6. Toss the apples with the chopped sage and a little ground black pepper. Spoon half of the lamb mixture into the pie dish. Top with half the apples and cover with another layer of lamb. Finish with a final layer of apple, piling up above the edge of the pie. Ease a pie funnel into the centre of the pie to help support the pastry and set aside.

Unwrap the pastry and roll it out into a large oval shape about 5cm larger than the pie dish. Cut a 2cm wide ring of pastry from around the edge of this oval. Brush the rim of the pie dish with the reserved egg mixture. Press the pastry ring on to the rim of the pie dish, overlapping slightly at the join. Brush lightly with a little more egg and then cover the pie completely with the rolled pastry, making a small hole for the top of the pie funnel.

to serve:
Serve the pie piping hot with creamy mashed potatoes and seasonal vegetables. Lightly cooked spinach goes very well with this.

Press the edges firmly to seal them together, then trim the pastry and flute all the way around. Brush the pastry with the remaining egg and put on a baking tray. Place in the centre of the oven and bake for 25 minutes or until the pastry is golden brown.

James Graham's Fillet of Zander
with duck eggs, asparagus and crayfish

Ask your fishmonger to scale and pinbone the fish.

Serves 2

2 zander cheeks
flour
1 egg, beaten
breadcrumbs
2 x 160g zander fillets, scaled and pinboned
olive oil
butter
3 duck egg yolks
8 spears of asparagus, trimmed and peeled
vegetable oil

Crayfish
8 large crayfish tails blanched and peeled
  (keep the heads for the stock)

olive oil
½ onion, diced
1 leek diced
2 carrots, peeled and diced
1 x 400g can chopped tomatoes
2g agar agar
50g butter

Almond foam
50g almond paste
100ml chicken stock
70ml semi-skimmed milk

To prepare the zander
Coat the zander cheeks in flour, dip into the beaten egg, then into the breadcrumbs, back into the egg and finally the breadcrumbs again. Set aside with the zander fillets.

To make the crayfish stock and jelly
Sauté the crayfish heads in a little olive oil until they turn red. Add the diced vegetables and sauté for 3 minutes. Add the tomatoes and enough water to cover – about 2 litres. Simmer for 50 minutes, strain, then put back in the pan and reduce to 400ml.

While the mixture is still hot, take 200ml and whisk in the agar agar. Pour into an ice cube tray to make 8 cubes and drop a crayfish tail into each one. Leave to set. Whisk the butter into the remaining 200ml of crayfish stock until you have a sauce consistency.

tip:
Zander is a delicious fish, with an exceptional texture and flavour so do give this a go.

To cook the duck eggs
Place the duck egg yolks in a bowl over a pan of simmering water and whisk until they register 60°C on a sugar thermometer. Cover and keep warm.

To make the almond foam

Place all the ingredients into a pan, bring to a simmer while whisking. When combined, set aside and keep warm. Just before serving, reheat gently (do not boil) and blend with a hand blender to create a foam.

To complete

Pan-fry the zander fillets, skin-side down, in a little oil and butter for 3 minutes. Turn over, cook for 2 minutes, then set aside in the pan somewhere warm to rest. Cook the asparagus until tender in boiling, salted water, drain and season. Heat the vegetable oil to 180°C in a deep-fat fryer and cook the zander cheeks until golden brown. Drain on kitchen paper.

To serve

Take two warm plates and spoon a slick of the duck egg yolk on each. Place some cubes of crayfish jelly on this and top with asparagus and zander cheek. Place the zander fillet to one side of the plate and drizzle with crayfish sauce. Finally, froth the almond foam and spoon it over the zander cheek.

Celebration of Gloucester Guinea Fowl
with apple risotto and baby leaf salad

Guinea fowl are under-used and under-rated in our opinion. They are similar to chicken but have a slightly gamey flavour and are well worth trying. We used our delicious Gloucestershire rapeseed oil in this dish, too.

Serves 4

tip: *The guinea fowl are jointed into breasts and thighs for this recipe so they can be cooked in different ways. Don't waste the carcasses – use them to make stock.*

Guinea fowl breasts

4 guinea fowl breasts
3 tbsp rapeseed oil
juice of ½ lime
zest of a lime
½ tsp sea salt flakes
1 tsp cracked black pepper
1 garlic clove, crushed
1 tsp thyme
110g smoked fatty streaky bacon,
cut into lardons

Guinea fowl thighs

125g basil, leaves picked from stems
125g rocket leaves
50g hard English cheese, freshly grated
75g dry-roasted pine nuts
2 garlic cloves, finely chopped
125ml rapeseed oil
8 guinea fowl thighs, boned
olive oil

Apple risotto

2 Cox's Pippins or Russet apples,
cut into 8
zest of 1 unwaxed lemon
75g butter
1.2–1.5 litres chicken stock
2 tbsp rapeseed oil
350g risotto rice
3 tbsp dry white wine
3 tbsp cloudy apple juice
3 sage leaves, chopped
3 tbsp freshly grated Parmesan cheese

Baby leaf salad

juice of an orange
2 tbsp lemon juice
2 tbsp white wine vinegar
1 garlic clove, crushed
pinch of English mustard powder
1 tsp soft brown sugar, or more to taste
baby salad leaves
3–5 tbsp rapeseed oil

To cook the guinea fowl breasts

Preheat the oven to 180°C/Gas 4. Slash the guinea fowl breasts in 3 or 4 places. In a pestle and mortar, mix 2 tablespoons of the rapeseed oil with the lime juice and zest, salt, black pepper, garlic and thyme and pound to a paste. Heat the remaining rapeseed oil in a frying pan, sauté the bacon lardons until crispy and the fat is running. Add the guinea fowl and sear on both sides to seal and give a little colour. Place the guinea fowl on a roasting tray, skin-side up, add the bacon and juices and paint on the zesty paste. Roast the breasts for 10–15 minutes until cooked, basting frequently. Take care not to overcook, as you want the breasts to be juicy. Leave to rest and reserve the resting juices and bacon lardons for the risotto.

To cook the guinea fowl thighs

Put the basil, rocket, cheese, pine nuts and garlic into a food processor and blitz to a purée. Add the rapeseed oil as you blitz until the mixture forms a thick, textured paste. The more oil you add, the looser the pesto becomes. Season to taste.

Open out the guinea fowl thighs and lay them on a chopping board, skin-side down. Spread a thin coating of the pesto on to the flesh. Roll the thighs up again to their former shape and secure with a couple of cocktail sticks. Brush with olive oil and season lightly. Place on a baking sheet and roast in the preheated oven for 30–35 minutes or until golden. Remove the cocktail sticks.

To make the apple risotto

Bring a pan of water to the boil. Add the apple segments and lemon zest and blanch for 3 minutes. Drain the apples and pat dry. Discard the zest. Melt 50g of the butter in a frying pan and fry the apples for about 5 minutes, stirring occasionally, until golden and caramelised. Remove from the heat and set aside.

Pour the stock into a saucepan and bring to a low boil. Heat another pan, add the rapeseed oil and the remaining butter, then pour in the rice and cook for a minute until all the grains of rice are coated in the oil. Add the white wine, stirring all the time until it evaporates, then add the apple juice. Add a ladleful of boiling hot stock to the rice and stir until it's absorbed. Repeat this process until all the stock has been absorbed into the rice. This should take about 20 minutes but you MUST KEEP STIRRING.

About 5 minutes before the end of the cooking time, when the rice is almost tender, add the apples, sage, Parmesan cheese and reserved bacon lardons and juices. Season to taste.

To prepare the baby leaf salad

Pour the orange juice into a jar, add the lemon juice, vinegar, garlic, mustard, and sugar and shake until combined. Adjust the seasoning. Dress the salad leaves first with the rapeseed oil, then add the dressing as you require. It is nice to show off the lovely vibrant yellow colour of the oil.

To serve

Slice the guinea fowl breasts and serve on warm plates with a couple of thighs, a spoonful of apple risotto and the salad.

County chef:
Peter Jackson
Restaurant:
Maes Y Neuadd

Peter Jackson is chef-proprietor at Maes Y Neuadd, which means 'the hall in the field'. It is a beautiful old manor house in the heart of the Snowdonia National Park and is surrounded by orchards and vegetable gardens, which offer an abundance of fresh produce. Peter is a leading light in the Welsh food world and has won many awards. He is also President of the Welsh Culinary Association and a founder member of the North Wales Chefs' Guild. He is passionate about seasonal produce and living off the land.

Gwynedd

"Gwynedd sheep are so lucky. They live in an area of outstanding natural beauty and graze on grass made sweet by the tangy sea air, so their meat is some of the best in the land. We went to see Dewi Owen's sheep farm and his animals looked as happy and healthy as you could wish for. There's a lot of good food in Gwynedd and one of the centres is the market town of Pwllheli, where we found the excellent Bwydlyn Butchers, Pwllheli Seafoods on the harbour, and the award-winning Spar, where they sell a huge range of food from local producers. We did our mobile kitchen in Portmeirion, an extraordinary Italian-style village perched on the coast. It was made famous as the location for a television series shown in the 1960s called 'The Prisoner'.

Then we met Cynan Jones, the mushroom man. He's a biker like us, and he loves mushrooms. He's managed to make his interest into a business and now makes a living gathering wild mushrooms and cultivating shiitake and oyster mushrooms in old shipping containers. "

Lobsgows

This is a kind of Welsh version of Irish stew and the marrow bones really give it a good rich flavour. Most butchers will give you the bones for nothing so don't be nervous about using them. We love sucking out the marrow. We know this is not everyone's idea of fun, but give it a go – it's scrumptious.

Serves 4–6

2–3 tbsp olive oil

1.2kg stewing beef, diced

2 marrow bones

1 onion, peeled and chopped

3 potatoes, peeled and chopped

1 swede, peeled and chopped

2 leeks, chopped

2 carrots, peeled and sliced

2 bay leaves

sea salt and pepper

1.5 litres beef stock, to cover

crusty bread

Preheat the oven to 150°C/Gas 2. Heat the olive oil in a large casserole dish and brown the diced beef. Add the marrow bones to the casserole and cook for 2–3 minutes, then remove the meat and bones from the dish and set aside.

Add the chopped onion to the dish and sweat for 1–2 minutes, then stir in the potatoes and swede. Cook for a further few minutes before adding the chopped leeks, carrots and bay leaves. Season to taste with salt and pepper and continue cooking for 1–2 minutes.

Put the beef and marrow bones back into the casserole and pour in enough of the beef stock to cover the meat. Cover with a lid, put in the oven and cook for 2½–3 hours or until the beef is tender. Serve with wedges of crusty bread.

the story of lobsgows:

Lobsgows is the Welsh version of stew eaten all over northern Europe. In Germany, it is known as labskaus and in Norway as lapskaus, and it may be made with fish as well as meat. Such stews were popular with seamen and so became associated with major seaports, such as Liverpool, where it is known as lobscouse or scouse – hence the name scouse or scousers for Liverpudlians.

Peter Jackson's Breast of Wild Duck
with warm duck brawn, smoked duck croquettes and sloe gin foam

The combination of these different ways of preparing duck is spectacular and ensures that you get the best from the different parts of the bird. The smoked duck croquettes also make a great starter on their own or can be served as nibbles with a glass of beer.

Serves 4

Duck breasts
4 breasts of wild duck or 2 duck breasts
vegetable oil
10g unsalted butter
1 shallot, chopped
a little finely chopped thyme
1 Granny Smith apple, peeled and cored
1 Conference pear, peeled and cored

Duck brawn
25g carrot, finely chopped
25g celery, finely chopped
25g leek, finely chopped
100ml chicken stock
50g confit of duck or cooked duck,
   finely chopped
10ml Madeira
1.5g gellan gum or agar agar

Smoked duck croquettes
50g confit of duck or cooked duck,
   finely chopped
100g mashed potatoes

25g shallot, carrot and swede,
   cooked and finely chopped
1 egg, beaten
50g breadcrumbs
50g fine oatmeal
25g flour

Sloe gin foam
50ml sloe gin
10ml duck stock
5ml olive oil
1g lecithin

Sauce
25g unsalted butter
1 shallot, finely chopped
1 tsp finely chopped thyme
25ml red wine
150ml dark duck stock

Garnish
dash of butternut squash purée

To prepare the duck breasts

Preheat the oven to 200°C/Gas 6. Season the duck breasts with salt and pepper and seal them in a hot frying pan with a little vegetable oil. Then place them in the hot oven for about 5 minutes. This should give a nice tender pink breast, depending on the size. Remove and leave to rest. Melt the butter, add the shallot and thyme and cook until soft without colouring. Chop the apple and pear, add them to the pan and cook until soft but not mushy. Season with salt and pepper and keep warm.

To prepare the duck brawn

Cook the vegetables in a little of the stock until al dente, then add the duck and the Madeira and reduce a little. Add the rest of the stock and warm to 40°C, then add the gellan gum or agar agar. Pour the liquid into 4 moulds and leave to set. When you're nearly ready to serve, place the moulds in a bain-marie and simmer gently for 25 minutes. Unmould on to the plates.

to serve:

Slice the duck breasts in half. Spoon some apple and pear mix on to the plate and top with duck breast. Add the warmed brawn and croquettes. Warm the butternut squash purée in a pan, spoon on to the plate and drag through it. Re-blend the foam and spoon a little over the side of the breast. Finish with

To prepare the smoked duck croquettes

Mix the duck, mash, vegetables and a little of the egg and shape into croquettes. Mix the breadcrumbs and oatmeal. Roll the croquettes through the flour and dip them in the rest of the beaten egg and then in the breadcrumbs. Deep-fry in hot oil until golden and keep warm.

To make the sloe gin foam

Warm the sloe gin, duck stock and oil to 60°C and leave to stand for 30 minutes. Pass the lecithin through a fine sieve and add to the liquid. Reheat to 60°C again and blitz with a hand blender to make foam. Do not heat to over 80°C as this breaks down the lecithin.

To make the sauce

Melt half the butter in a pan, add the shallot and thyme and soften without colouring. Add the red wine and reduce by half and then add the stock and reduce by half again. Finish with

Trio of Welsh Lamb
with three-root vegetable mash and buttered kale

The lamb in Gwynedd was so good that we wanted to try different ways of showing it off. The confit of lamb can be cooked for 12 hours or more – just make sure it is tightly sealed in foil. Mutton is good cooked this way, too.

Serves 6–8

Confit shoulder of lamb

3 tbsp olive oil
1 small shoulder of lamb
½ head of garlic
2 sprigs of rosemary, chopped
3 chopped anchovies
100ml white wine
splash of port
knob of butter

Lamb adobe

knob of butter
250g oyster mushrooms, chopped
125g shiitake mushrooms, chopped
20g dried ceps, rehydrated in hot water
1 onion, peeled and finely chopped
1 small handful of flat-leaf parsley,
  chopped
1 tsp red wine vinegar
pinch of sugar
250g thin streaky bacon, rind removed
1 whole lamb loin fillet, trimmed

Rack of lamb

1 rack of lamb, French trimmed
2 tbsp Dijon mustard
100g white breadcrumbs
1 small handful of parsley, chopped
1 small handful of mint, chopped
1 tsp chopped rosemary
3 garlic cloves, peeled and crushed
olive oil

Three-root vegetable mash

500g celeriac, peeled
500g potatoes, peeled
500g Jerusalem artichokes, peeled
3–4 tbsp double cream
knob of butter

Kale

200g kale, finely shredded
knob of butter

sprigs of rosemary for garnish

To prepare the confit shoulder of lamb

tip:
All meat should be at room temperature when you start to cook it, so take it out of the fridge in good time.

Preheat the oven to 150°C/Gas 2. Heat the olive oil in a roasting tray, season the lamb shoulder with sea salt and freshly ground black pepper and brown it all over in the roasting tray. Add the garlic to the tray and scatter the chopped rosemary and anchovies over the lamb. Pour in the white wine, wrap the tray in a double layer of foil and roast in the oven for 6 hours. Remove the meat from the bone, shred it with your fingers or a fork and set aside.

Strain the cooking juices into a pan, add a splash of port and boil until reduced. Whisk in a knob of butter and heat gently to keep the sauce warm. Pack the shredded meat into suitable chef's rings and place on a baking tray. Just before serving, warm the confit through in the oven.

To prepare the lamb adobe

Heat a knob of butter in a pan and sauté the mushrooms for a few minutes to soften them. Remove from the heat and put them into a blender. Drain the dried ceps (reserve the liquid), chop them finely and add to the blender with the onion, chopped parsley, red wine vinegar and sugar. Blend until smooth, adding any reserved mushroom liquid if needed to loosen the mixture. Heat a drizzle of oil in a pan and sauté the mushroom mixture for a few minutes to soften.

Place the bacon rashers on a chopping board lined with clingfilm. Using the back of a knife, stretch the rashers out to make them thinner. Preheat the oven to 180°C/Gas 4. Place the rashers side by side, slightly overlapping each other, and spread a thin layer of the mushroom mixture over them. Season with sea salt and black pepper. Place the lamb loin on top and wrap it up tightly using the clingfilm to help you. You can twist the ends to get a really tight, neat shape. Remove the clingfilm, making sure the bacon rasher ends are well tucked in. Place the lamb on a roasting tray and roast for 15–20 minutes for pink meat, 20 minutes for medium and 25 minutes for well down. Remove and leave to rest for 5–10 minutes.

to serve:

Spoon the mash into a piping bag and pipe on to the plates. Carve the lamb loin into slices, and arrange on top of the mash. Spoon the kale alongside it. Cut the lamb rack into cutlets and arrange on top of the kale. Finally, place the confit lamb shoulder on the plate, garnish with a rosemary and pour the sauce over the confit.

To prepare the rack of lamb

Preheat the oven to 180°C/Gas 4. Score the fat with a knife and brown the rack in a hot pan for a few minutes. Remove and brush the rack all over with Dijon mustard. Mix the breadcrumbs, chopped parsley, mint, rosemary, garlic, seasoning and a glug of olive oil together in a bowl. Spoon this mixture over the lamb and press it down carefully. Put the lamb in a roasting tray and roast for 20–25 minutes. Remove and leave to rest.

To prepare the three-root mash and the kale

Chop the celeriac, potatoes and Jerusalem artichokes to a similar size so they all cook in the same time. Boil until soft. Drain, then place in a blender with the cream and seasoning and blitz until smooth. Transfer to a pan with a touch of butter and allow to warm through. Blanch the kale in a pan of boiling salted water for 2 minutes. Drain and season to taste. Before serving, toss with a knob of butter and warm through.

County chef:
Alex Aitken
Restaurant:
Le Poussin

A self-taught chef, Alex Aitken earned the New Forest's first Michelin star in 1994. Le Poussin is part of his country house hotel, Whitley Ridge in the New Forest, and has won a number of other accolades. Alex loves to use wild ingredients, as well as local produce, whenever he can.

He's a keen fungi forager and has found summer truffles and other rarities in the land around the hotel. He's won praise from chef Gordon Ramsay who said of his meal at Le Poussin: 'It's like eating off the forest floor, especially in the mushroom season.' Ramsay also enjoyed the game and puddings.

Hampshire

Hampshire is a county of contrasts – the southern coasts and northern heathland, the valleys and the forests. It is at the heart of England and in fact, Winchester was once the capital. Now, Winchester has a farmers' market that is one of the biggest and best in Britain and all produce for sale in the market must come from Hampshire or within ten miles of the border. We noticed something here that we've seen in other counties too – foods that go well together often come from the same place. For example, Hampshire is a major grower of watercress, which goes superbly with one of its other important foods – trout. Both are products of the wonderfully pure chalk streams of this county.

We were thrilled to meet former Formula 1 World Champion Jody Scheckter who now runs Laverstoke Park Farm. He's done masses of research on creating the perfect biodynamic relationship between soil and livestock or crop. He has two sites, one for animals and one for fruit and veg, and aims to produce the best-tasting, healthiest foods. And then there was the wonderful Mrs Tee, who has been picking mushrooms from the New Forest since 1972. Her fungi knowledge is such that chefs from Buckingham Palace have come to her for advice.

Trout en Papillote

Cooking 'en papillote' is so easy and preserves all the natural flavours of the food. Another good thing to cook this way is wild mushrooms – add butter and seasoning to a handful, wrap them up and let them cook in their own steam.

Serves 4

50g butter

4 whole trout, cleaned

1 large bunch of dill

1 large bunch of flat-leaf parsley

1 large bunch of chervil

2 lemons, sliced

2 bunches of watercress

700g new potatoes, scrubbed

Preheat the oven to 220°C/Gas 7. You will need 4 large sheets of baking parchment. Place a knob of butter, then a trout on to one of the sheets. Put some dill, parsley and chervil in the cavity of the trout, along with a few slices of lemon. Season well with salt and black pepper and top with some watercress. Fold the parchment over the trout and turn the edges over to secure them. Make the other 3 parcels in the same way and place them all on a baking sheet. Put them into the preheated oven and cook for 15–20 minutes. Put the potatoes into a pan of salted water, bring to the boil and simmer for 10–12 minutes or until tender. Drain and toss with the rest of the butter, salt and black pepper.

Smoked Trout and Watercress Salad

Serves 4

600g smoked trout fillet

2 large bunches of watercress

110g walnuts, shelled

2 pears, cut into cubes

1 tbsp white wine vinegar

3 tbsp rapeseed oil

1 tbsp honey

2 tsp grainy mustard

1 tbsp horseradish cream

3 tbsp crème fraîche

Flake the smoked trout into large pieces and pick the leaves off the watercress. Toss both lightly with the walnuts and pears. Pour the vinegar, oil and honey into a jam jar, season with salt and black pepper and shake vigorously until well mixed. Drizzle the dressing over the salad and toss once more very lightly. Mix the mustard, horseradish and crème fraîche together and serve with the salad.

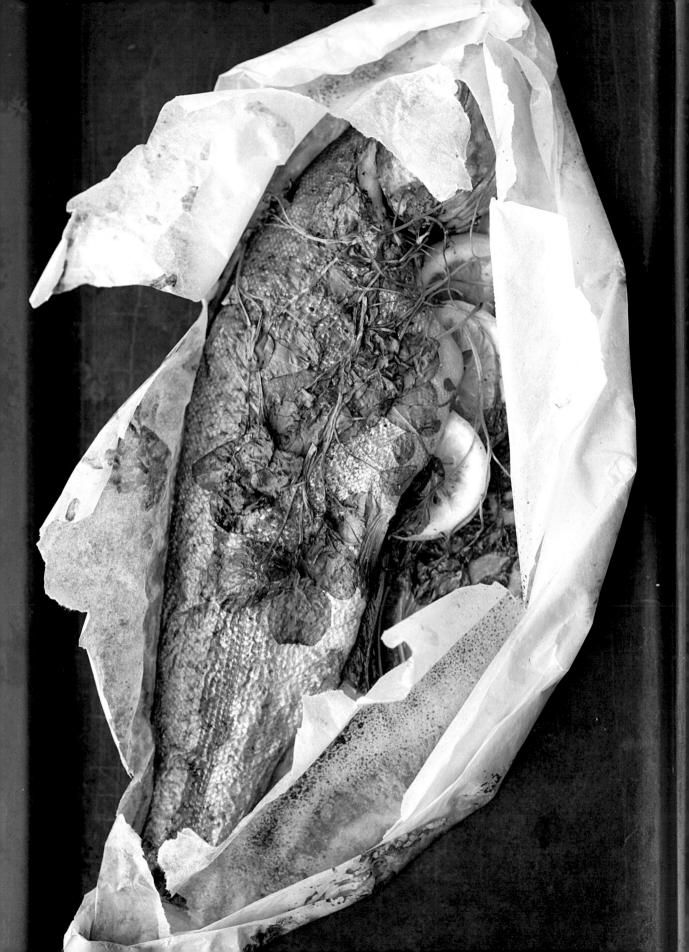

Alex Aitken's saddle of New Forest Venison

with poached pears, caramelised walnuts and fondant potatoes

Venison is a wonderful meat and very popular in the New Forest area. When cooking the fillets, don't overcrowd the pan. If the pieces of meat are too packed together they will steam, not sear and the flavour won't be right – something to remember when searing or browning any kind of meat. Also, with very lean meat like venison it is important to keep basting it as it cooks to keep it juicy and tender.

Serves 4

Venison
olive oil
butter
4 loin fillets of venison, trimmed
    (keep the trimmings for the sauce)

Sauce and haggis
venison trimmings, cut into small pieces
olive oil
butter
1 shallot and 1 carrot, finely chopped
110g redcurrant jelly
110ml red wine vinegar
500ml venison stock or 200ml reduced
    stock
4 New Forest venison haggis, cooked

Caramelised walnuts
150g caster sugar
150ml water
150g walnut halves

Poached pear
1 pear (not too ripe)
1 cinnamon stick
1 star anise
5 peppercorns
1 strip of orange zest
250ml red wine
pinch of sugar

Fondant potatoes
4 large potatoes
250g butter (or enough to nearly
    cover the potatoes in the pan)
1 sprig of thyme
1 garlic clove

Swede and cabbage
1 large swede
butter
black pepper
1 small savoy cabbage

To prepare the venison

Heat a large frying pan and add a little olive oil and butter. Season the loin fillets and add them to the pan. (It is important to use a large pan so that the venison sizzles and browns – if the pan is too small the temperature will drop too much and the meat will not sear.) When the meat is seared, baste it with a little more butter and cook for 3–4 minutes on each side, turning and basting frequently. Leave the meat to rest on a warm dish with the cooking juices.

To prepare the sauce and haggis

Brown the venison trimmings in a hot pan with a little olive oil and butter. Add the shallot and carrot and cook until they are softened and browned. Add the redcurrant jelly and allow it to melt, and then pour in the red wine vinegar. Reduce to a glaze, then add the venison stock and reduce to a rich sauce. Strain the sauce through a fine sieve and keep it warm until ready to serve. Place the haggis in a saucepan, add a small amount of the strained sauce and gently heat it through.

To prepare the caramelised walnuts

Put the sugar and water in a saucepan, add the walnuts and cook slowly until all the water has gone. Turn the caramelised walnuts on to a non-stick surface and leave to cool.

to serve:

Arrange a portion of the buttered cabbage in the centre of each plate. Add a spoonful of swede, some fondant potatoes and a haggis. Add a quarter of the pear, and a few caramelised walnuts. Slice the venison and arrange it on top of the cabbage. Drizzle the sauce over and around

To prepare the poached pear

Peel the pear and cut it into quarters, removing the core. Put the quarters and all the other ingredients in a small high-sided saucepan and cook gently until the pear is just tender. Turn up the heat towards the end to glaze the pear.

To make the fondant potatoes

Peel the potatoes and cut with a cookie cutter to a uniform size – this ensures that they cook evenly. Melt the butter with thyme and garlic in a frying pan (use enough to nearly cover the potatoes in the pan), add the potatoes and cook slowly so they soften and absorb the butter.

To prepare the swede and cabbage

Cook the swede and purée it with butter. Season with black pepper. Chop the cabbage, cook

Roast Belly of Pork
with wild boar and mushroom tortellini

Make sure that the skin of the pork is properly dry before you add the herbs and salt, and really rub the salty mixture in well for a crisp skin. When preparing the tortellini, don't overstuff them, or they will fall apart when cooking.

Serves 4

1kg belly pork, boneless
4 bay leaves
1 tbsp Maldon sea salt
2 tsp black peppercorns
4 garlic cloves

Tortellini

200g Italian tipo 00 flour
1 egg
6 egg yolks
250g wild boar loin, trimmed and roughly chopped
75g pork fat, roughly chopped
2 tbsp olive oil
½ onion, finely chopped
1 garlic clove, crushed
150g wild mushrooms, trimmed
75ml fresh beef stock
1 egg, beaten
50g butter
1 tbsp truffle oil
2 tbsp chervil, roughly chopped

Red wine sauce

200ml red wine
5 juniper berries
3 sage leaves
1 sprig of rosemary
1cm of root ginger, peeled
½ Bramley apple, peeled and chopped
200ml fresh beef stock
3 tbsp redcurrant jelly
50g butter

To prepare the belly pork

Preheat the oven to 180°C/Gas 4. Score the fat on the belly into diamonds, and slash the meat with a sharp knife. Pour boiling water over the pork, fat side up, then pat it dry. Discard the water. Crush the bay leaves, salt, black peppercorns and garlic to a rough paste in a pestle and mortar and rub this into both sides of the pork belly. Place the meat on a rack over a roasting tray, cover with foil and place in the oven for 2 hours. At the end of this time, turn the oven up to 230°C/Gas 8. Remove the foil and return the pork to the oven for another 15 minutes to crisp up the skin. Alternatively, you can finish the crackling under a hot grill. Leave to rest for 15 minutes.

To make the tortellini

Pour the flour into a bowl, make a well in the centre and add the egg and egg yolks. Gradually draw the mixture together and knead for 2 minutes to make a soft dough. Cover and leave it to rest in the fridge for 30 minutes.

Put the wild boar and the pork fat into a food processor and blitz to a purée. Heat a frying pan, add a tablespoon of the olive oil, the onion and garlic and sauté for 1–2 minutes until the onion is just softened. Add the wild boar purée and cook for 3–4 minutes more. Roughly chop one-third of the mushrooms.

Heat a separate frying pan, add some of the oil and the chopped mushrooms and fry for 2 minutes until any liquid has evaporated. Add the wild boar mixture, then pour in the stock and simmer for 3–4 minutes. Season with salt and black pepper, then set aside to cool.

Divide the pasta into 2 pieces. Pass these through a pasta machine, gradually reducing the thickness until the pasta feels elastic and the machine is on the finest setting. Cut the pasta into 7.5cm circles and brush with the beaten egg. Place a small spoonful of filling to one side of the circle. Roll the pasta up into a tube and then around to make a ring. Repeat until all the pasta and filling is used up, then set the tortellini aside until ready to serve.

Bring a pan of salted water to the boil. Drop in the tortellini and boil for a couple of minutes until they float to the surface. Remove the tortellini and toss them with a little butter and truffle oil, then season with salt and black pepper. Heat a frying pan, add the remaining butter, olive oil and mushrooms and sauté for 2 minutes until just cooked. Season with salt and black pepper and toss in the chervil. Keep warm.

To make the red wine sauce

Pour the red wine into a saucepan, add the juniper berries, sage, rosemary, ginger and apple and bring to the boil. Turn the heat down and simmer until reduced by half. Remove the ginger and add the stock and redcurrant jelly. Bring back to the boil and simmer until reduced by half again. Season with salt and black pepper, then whisk in the butter. Strain the sauce and keep warm until ready to serve.

To serve

Cut the pork belly into squares. Place some mushrooms in a pile on the centre of each plate and top with a piece of pork. Place the tortellini around the mushrooms. Spoon the sauce over the tortellini and around the plate. Serve immediately.

County chef:
James Arbourne
Restaurant:
The Bridge at Wilton

James Arbourne was born and bred in Herefordshire. The Bridge, which he has run for four years, is recommended in the Michelin Guide, has two AA rosettes and has also won the 'Flavours of Herefordshire Restaurant of the Year' award three years running. James loves his county and is hugely proud of its food. He is very involved with the farming community and believes that Herefordshire produces the best meat, dairy food and vegetables available. The soufflé on page 124 is one of his signature dishes.

Herefordshire

"On our travels around Britain we discovered that we are a nation obsessed with beef and cheese. People are passionate about them. We visited at least six different beef producers and while they were all excellent, the beef from the Hereford cattle did stand out as one of the best. The taste is just amazing – so different from supermarket beef. We loved our time in this county. As travellers in a rural land, we got a really traditional country welcome and warm hospitality. Herefordshire is an immensely fertile area and the Wye Valley in particular produces a wide range of quality fruit and vegetables.

We met some wonderful food producers. People like Jo Hilditch, whose family have been growing blackcurrants since the 1930s and supplied them to Ribena. A few years back, Jo decided to try making cassis and it's the best we've ever tasted. The balance of sweetness and acidity is perfect and we'll be going back for more. Then there was Tony Vaughan who runs L'Escargot Anglais. Back in the 1980s, he spotted a market for top-quality British snails and now turns out four tonnes a year and supplies some of London's top chefs with his plump, tender beauties. "

Roast Herefordshire Beef
with homemade creamed horseradish

Of all the mobile kitchen dishes we made, this was the one people went most bonkers about. They loved it and rightly so – perfect beef, tasty horseradish, caramelised onions. The people of Herefordshire couldn't get enough!

Serves 6–8

Beef

1 tbsp vegetable oil

½ whole sirloin

2 tbsp English mustard powder

1 tbsp ground sea salt

1 tbsp cracked black pepper

Rolls and trimmings

big knob of butter

2 tbsp olive oil

1kg onions, peeled and sliced

12–16 bread rolls, split in half

4 little gem lettuces, leaves separated

Creamed horseradish

4 tbsp horseradish root, grated

1 tbsp white wine vinegar

pinch of English mustard powder

1 tsp caster sugar

150ml double cream

Meat thermometer guide

45°C for rare
50°C for medium-rare
60°C for medium
68°C for medium well-done
72°C for well-done

Don't forget – the temperature will go up about 10 degrees while the meat rests.

to serve:

Slice the beef thickly. The end pieces can go to the people who like beef well done. Dip half a roll into the cooking fat and juices, pile on a couple of slices of beef, then top with fried onions and lettuce. On the other half of the roll, spread the lovely creamed horseradish, place on top and serve.

To cook the beef

Preheat the oven to 220°C/Gas 7. Heat the vegetable oil in a roasting tin and seal the sirloin all over, including the ends, then set aside. Mix together the mustard, salt and pepper, and rub it into the sirloin. Do it with feeling – this is a great piece of meat.

Now, rules for roasting. Put the beef in the preheated oven for 30 minutes to roast. Then lower the temperature to 160°/Gas 3 and continue to roast. The time depends on how you like your beef. For rare, and this is what we did, cook for 20 minutes per kilo. For medium beef, cook for 30 minutes per kilo. For well done, 40 minutes per kilo.

To test that the meat is perfectly cooked, use a meat thermometer. Place the spike into the centre of the meat and check the reading. The meat is ready when the reading is 10 degrees below the desired temperature – see the note at the side of this page. Remove the meat from the oven and leave it to rest somewhere warm for 15 minutes. During the resting time the meat continues to cook inside so will reach the required temperature within the 15 minutes.

We like to eat this great beef rare so our required temperature is 45°C. That means taking it out of the oven when the meat thermometer shows 35°–40°.

To prepare the trimmings and horseradish

Heat the butter and the olive oil in a big frying pan. Fry the sliced onions until they are golden brown and your house smells like a burger van. Make the creamed horseradish by mixing everything together until thickened.

James Arbourne's Best End of Phocle Green Pork

with Hereford hop cheese soufflé and Broome Farm perry jus

With top-quality free-range pork like this you don't have to worry about cooking it right through. It's fine to serve the meat slightly pink and it will be tender and delicious.

Serves 4

Pork

1 medium banana shallot,
    peeled and roughly chopped
1 carrot, peeled and roughly chopped
1 celery stick, peeled and
    roughly chopped
½ leek, peeled and roughly chopped
olive oil
500ml Herefordshire perry
300ml Herefordshire pear juice
300ml reduced pork stock
4 larder-trimmed pork cutlets,
    about 150g each, wrapped in
    cured ham
knob of butter

Pears

4 pears
50ml stock syrup
200ml Herefordshire perry
110ml Herefordshire pear juice
4tsp cider vinegar
sugar (optional)

Soufflé

olive oil
50g fresh breadcrumbs, mixed with 10g
    chopped toasted hops
150g Hereford hop cheese, grated
175ml milk
60g strong white flour
200g free-range egg whites
1 tsp lemon juice
8 small cubes of Hereford hop cheese

Vegetables

3 medium-sized Estima potatoes,
    peeled and cubed
140g Herefordshire unsalted butter
150g swede, carrot and parsnip
    peeled and diced
8 small stems of purple-sprouting broccoli
1 tsp light olive oil infused with thyme
sea salt, freshly ground white pepper
    and caster sugar to taste

Preheat the oven to 110°C/Gas ¼. Caramelise the chopped shallot, carrot, celery and leek in a little olive oil. Add the perry and pear juice and reduce to a syrupy liquid. Add the reduced pork stock, simmer for 1 minute, then check for seasoning and sweetness and add salt and/or sugar as necessary. Pan-fry the pork cutlets in olive oil until golden on both sides. Add a knob of butter and baste, then place in the oven for 4 minutes. Take out and leave to rest in the pan.

To cook the pears

Cut the pears in half. Take 1 thin slice from the centre of each, then peel, core and chop the rest. Coat each thin pear slice in stock syrup and place on siliconised paper. Place in a low oven (110°C/Gas ¼) for 3 hours until crisp. Put the chopped pear, perry, pear juice and cider vinegar in a pan and cook over a low heat until jam-like. Add sugar if necessary.

To make the soufflés

Preheat the oven to 190°C/Gas 5. Coat the insides of 4 dariole moulds with olive oil and then dredge with the breadcrumb and hop mixture making sure the surfaces are well covered. Spread the flour thinly and evenly on a baking tray and bake for 5 minutes.

Put the cheese and 150ml of the milk in a medium saucepan and cook slowly until the cheese has melted. Add the cooked flour, season and stir vigorously, then after 1 minute remove from the heat. The mixture will be very thick. Mix in the rest of the milk to loosen the mixture.

Beat the egg whites with a pinch of salt until frothy, then add the lemon juice and continue beating until firm. Carefully fold the egg whites into the cheese mixture. Ladle the soufflé mixture into the darioles until they are half full. Place 2 cubes of cheese in each dariole, then fill to the top with the remaining mixture.

Place the darioles in a baking tray and pour boiling water into the tray to come one-third of the way up the sides of the moulds. Bake in the preheated oven for 6 minutes, then turn the tray and cook for another 6 minutes. The soufflés should be firm to the touch. Allow the soufflés to cool slightly, then tip them out of the darioles on to a baking tray.

To prepare the vegetables

Gently poach the potatoes in salted water. Drain them well, mash and push through a drum sieve. Mix in half the butter and season to taste. Sweat the diced root vegetables in the remaining butter and season with salt, white pepper and a little caster sugar. When they are soft, crush with a masher, taste and adjust the seasoning if necessary. Boil the broccoli in salted water for 1 minute, drain and season with infused olive oil, salt and pepper.

to serve:

Place a mound of mashed potatoes on each plate, with the broccoli on top. Add the pork. Pop the soufflés back into the oven for 2 minutes. Spoon the crushed roots on to the plate and top with a soufflé. Sandwich the pear jam in between 2 pear crisps, add to the plate and drizzle the pork sauce around.

Snail-topped Hereford Fillet of Beef

with snail beignets, straw potatoes, and red wine and cassis sauce

We used Tony Vaughan's little beauties, which come ready purged, for our dish. If you gather your own wall fish, as they are sometimes called, you'll need to purge them yourself. Just put them in a bucket with some bran and leave them until the bran starts to come out the other end! Then you know they are thoroughly clean.

Serves 4

Snail topping

125g melted butter
1 shallot, finely chopped
2 garlic cloves, crushed
2 tbsp chopped parsley
meat from 24 snails,
finely chopped
25g breadcrumbs
4 slices of white bread
knob of butter and 1 tbsp olive oil

Beef

4 barrelled fillet steaks
1 tbsp vegetable oil
butter

Snail beignets

vegetable oil
20 snails, roughly chopped
1 tbsp olive oil
3 tbsp chopped herbs: parsley,
thyme, tarragon and chervil
50g butter
75g plain flour
2 eggs

Straw potatoes

1kg seasonal potatoes, peeled

Red wine and cassis sauce

200ml full-bodied red wine
50ml port
6 juniper berries
1 bay leaf
500ml beef demi-glace
1 tbsp cassis
75g butter

Spinach and garlic

1 head of garlic
1 tbsp olive oil
big knob of butter
250g spinach

To prepare the snail topping and beef

Mix the butter, shallot, garlic, parsley, snails and breadcrumbs in a bowl and season with salt and pepper. Spread this mixture on a sheet of silicon baking parchment on a baking tray and then put in the fridge to cool and set. Using a pastry cutter roughly the same size as the steaks, cut out 4 rounds of snail topping. Heat the oil and butter in a frying pan and cut out 4 rounds of bread with the pastry cutter. Fry the bread in the oil and butter to make golden croutons.

Preheat the oven to 220°C/Gas 7. Make sure the steaks are at room temperature. Take a heavy frying pan, the kind with a handle you can put in the oven. Heat the oil to smoking in the pan and sear the steaks on all sides until brown. Add some butter and spoon it over the top of the steak.

Place a round of snail topping on each steak and place them in the oven for 5–8 minutes, until the snail butter is sizzling and the steak is cooked rare. Place the steaks on the croutons – the bread is more than decorative as it will absorb the meat juices and garlic butter from the snails. Leave to rest for 5 minutes before serving.

To make the snail beignets

Heat the oil in a deep-fat fryer to 180°C. Put the snails in a bowl with the olive oil and mixed herbs and leave to marinate for 1 hour. Pour 125ml of water into a saucepan, add the butter and bring to the boil. Simmer until all the butter has melted, then beat in the flour. Cook for 3–4 minutes until the flour has cooked out, then remove from the heat. Beat in the eggs, one by one, until smooth and glossy. Add the marinated snails, season with salt and black pepper and mix well. Drop spoonfuls of the mixture into the fryer a few at a time and fry until golden and puffed up. Drain on kitchen paper .

To make the straw potatoes

Heat the deep-fat fryer to 160°C. Using the mandolin set to 3mm julienne, reduce the potatoes to a pile of sticks. Rinse them in a couple of changes of water to wash out the starch. When the water is clear, blot the sticks dry on kitchen paper and spread them out on a tea towel to dry for 15 minutes. Take a handful of potato sticks and squeeze lightly into a ball or whatever shape you like. Fry until golden and season with sea salt.

To make the red wine and cassis sauce

Pour the red wine and port into a pan and add the juniper berries and bay leaf. Simmer until reduced by half. Add the stock and reduce again until it has the required consistency and strength of taste. Remove the bay leaf and the juniper berries and discard. Add the cassis and whisk in the butter.

To prepare the spinach and garlic

Preheat the oven to 180°C/Gas 4. Top and tail the head of garlic. Pour on the olive oil and roast in the oven for about 15 minutes or until the garlic cloves are soft. In a frying pan melt the butter and add the spinach. Cook until the spinach is just wilted, then season with salt and black pepper.

To serve

Place a beef stack on the centre of each plate. Squeeze a clove of roasted garlic on top. Serve some spinach alongside it and a beignet. Add some straw potatoes and spoon the sauce around.

County chef:
David Pitchford
Restaurant:
Read's

Read's is set in an elegant Georgian manor house near Faversham and is surrounded by beautiful grounds. Its excellent reputation is well deserved and it has held a Michelin star for 17 years. Chef-proprietor David Pitchford is a grand master of British cooking and we learned so much from him.

He was incredibly good to us enthusiastic amateurs – even when we almost wrecked his kitchen trying to fry bladderwrack! Cooking with him was a dream come true. David serves wonderful food and many of his herbs and vegetables come from his walled kitchen garden.

Kent

"Traditionally known as the garden of England, Kent still produces lots of great food. We went to the best farmers' market in Canterbury, called the Goods Shed, where local farmers and other suppliers can sell their produce seven days a week. Food critic Jay Rayner describes it as 'pure gastro-porn' and he's right. Amazing place. One day we went out with forager Fergus Drennan. He earns a living gathering wild food, such as seaweeds and wild mushrooms, and knows an incredible amount about local wild plants. We also had a great visit to Shepherd Neame, Britain's oldest brewery. They grow hops in Kent, of course, and we've never tasted such deliciously hoppy beer."

Kentish Cobnut Cake
with apple compote

Cobnuts used to be an important crop in Kent and a staple food for many. They keep well, so people found ways of using them, including this traditional cake. Apples are another local ingredient and a great accompaniment.

Serves 4

Cake	Apple compote
450g self-raising flour	50g butter
225g butter, melted	4 apples, peeled, cored and
1 tbsp ground ginger	finely chopped
225g soft light-brown sugar	2–3 tbsp caster sugar
6 eggs, beaten	½ tsp ground cinnamon
110g double cream	200ml double cream,
150g cobnuts, shelled and finely chopped	lightly whipped, for serving

To make the cake
Preheat the oven to 160°C/Gas 3. Pour the flour into a bowl and stir in the melted butter. Add the ground ginger, sugar and eggs and mix together. Pour in the cream and stir well to make a thick batter. Add the cobnuts and stir so they are well mixed into the batter. Spoon into a buttered 1kg loaf tin, making sure the mixture settles into all the corners.

Bake for 1–1¼ hours until golden and cooked through. Check by inserting a skewer into the centre of the cake – if it comes out sticky, then cook the cake for another 10 minutes. Allow the cake to cool slightly in the tin, then turn out and serve warm.

To prepare the compote
Heat a frying pan, add the butter, apples, caster sugar and cinnamon and cook for 4–5 minutes until the apples are tender and slightly broken down.

To serve
Slice the cake and serve with a dollop of cream and a spoonful of apple compote.

David Pitchford's Celebration of Kent Lamb

This is really four recipes in one and all are great. Try one a week – will keep you happy for a month!

Serves 4

Individual shepherd's pies
200g braising lamb
500ml chicken stock
450g potatoes
2 tbsp double cream
25g butter, melted
1 egg yolk

Loin of lamb with courgettes Provençale
1 boned loin of lamb
1 shallot, finely chopped
1 garlic clove, finely chopped
25ml olive oil
4 Italian plum tomatoes, blanched and skinned
2 courgettes, diced

Rump of lamb with buttered flageolet beans
200g dried flageolet beans, soaked overnight in cold water
500ml chicken stock
200g rump of lamb
25ml olive oil
25g butter, melted

Lambs' kidneys and fillet with fresh leaf spinach
1 fillet of lamb, fully trimmed
2 lambs' kidneys
25ml olive oil
200g fresh leaf spinach, washed, stalks removed
25g butter

Rosemary jus
1 litre lamb stock
250ml Cabernet Sauvignon red wine
2 sprigs of fresh rosemary, leaves chopped

To make the shepherd's pies
Gently poach the lamb in the chicken stock for about 1 hour. Wash, peel and rewash the potatoes, place them in a pan of salted water and boil until tender. Drain and return to the pan over the heat to drive off the moisture. Mash well, then add the double cream, melted butter and the egg yolk.

When the lamb is cooked, remove it from the stock and dice. Reduce the stock in which the meat has been cooked, add this to the diced meat and spoon into 4 small individual pie dishes. Using a piping bag and nozzle, pipe the potato on to the meat and glaze under a preheated grill.

To prepare the loin of lamb and courgettes

Season the loin of lamb, then pan-fry it for 6–8 minutes and leave to rest. Heat a frying pan and sweat the shallot and garlic in half the olive oil. Chop the tomatoes and add them to the pan. Simmer, stirring occasionally, until most of the juice has evaporated. In a separate pan, lightly fry the courgettes in the remaining oil, then drain them and add to the tomato sauce. Check the seasoning.

To prepare the rump of lamb and flageolet beans

Drain the beans and simmer in chicken stock until tender. Trim and remove the skin from the rump of lamb, then season. Heat the olive oil in a frying pan, then add the lamb and cook for 10–15 minutes until pink. Remove it from the pan and leave to rest for 5 minutes. Toss the beans in melted butter and season.

to serve:

Spoon the courgettes on to the serving plates, slice the loin of lamb and arrange on top. Spoon the beans on to the plates and cut two slices of rump per portion to place on top of the beans. Add a portion of spinach with the sliced fillet and one half of kidney on top. Spoon the jus over the plated loin, rump and kidney and serve with a shepherd's pie on the side.

To prepare the lambs' kidneys and fillet and fresh leaf spinach

Remove the fat and sinew from the fillet of lamb. Slice the kidneys lengthways and remove the outside membrane and the white gristle from the centre. Season the fillet and kidneys with salt and black pepper. Heat a frying pan, add the olive oil and fry the lamb fillet and kidneys for 4–5 minutes, until just pink. Cook the spinach briefly in boiling water, drain, season and toss in butter.

To prepare the rosemary jus

Pour the lamb stock into a pan and bring to the boil. Lower the heat slightly and cook until the liquid is reduced by two-thirds. Add the red wine and reduce again by half. Use this stock to deglaze the cooking pans when the lamb has been cooked and add any meat juices from the resting meat. Add the rosemary leaves to the sauce and gently simmer for 5 minutes. Pass it through a fine strainer and check the seasoning.

Dover Sole
and Beer Sabayon
with seaweed and pommes noisettes

The seaweed we gathered with Fergus was so tasty and went perfectly with this delicious Dover sole. Just don't do what we did and try to fry bladderwrack – it's a blood sport! Use curly kale instead.

Serves 8

Dover sole
4 tbsp plain flour
½ tsp smoked paprika
8 fillets of Dover sole, skinned
2 eggs, beaten
2 tbsp olive oil
50g butter

Beer sabayon
110ml wheat beer
3 large egg yolks
1 tsp lemon juice
2–3 tbsp chopped chives

Pommes noisettes
1kg waxy potatoes, peeled
50g butter
1 tbsp olive oil
4 tbsp chopped sea purslane

Seaweed and kale
1kg sea beet leaves
50g butter
500g sea alexander,
   leaves discarded
vegetable oil
200g curly kale, finely sliced

To cook the Dover sole
Mix the flour with some salt, black pepper and paprika. Dip the fish in beaten egg, then dredge in the seasoned flour. Heat a large frying pan, add the oil and butter and fry the fish for 1–2 minutes on each side, until golden and just cooked. Set aside on a warm plate.

To prepare the beer sabayon
Pour one-third of the beer into a heatproof bowl, add the egg yolks and whisk together. Place the bowl over a pan of boiling water, so it sits just above the water level. Continue to whisk for a couple of minutes until the sabayon starts to thicken, then add the remaining beer and whisk some more. Turn off the heat and continue to whisk. Once the sabayon thickens, add the lemon juice and chives, season, and whisk again for 30 seconds or so.

tip:
Treat the sabayon carefully so you don't end up with scrambled eggs. Ideally, place the bowl on the pan just before the water boils, then increase the heat very gently.

To prepare the pommes noisettes
Preheat the oven to 200°C/Gas 6. Using a melon baller or parisienne scoop, cut out lots of little round balls of potato – you need about 12 per portion. Heat a large frying pan, add the butter and oil and fry the potato balls, stirring constantly.

Once they have taken on some colour, place them in the oven on a baking tray and roast for 5–8 minutes until golden and tender. Add the chopped sea purslane and season with salt and black pepper.

To cook the seaweed and kale
Bring a large pan of salted water to the boil. Add the sea beet leaves, cook for 1–2 minutes, then drain and refresh. Put them in a blender with the butter and blitz to a purée, adding a little cooking water if necessary. Pass the purée through a sieve into a pan, ready to reheat before serving. Trim the ends from the sea alexander and peel. Bring a pan of salted water to the boil, add the sea alexander and cook for 1–2 minutes. Drain and refresh, then toss in a hot pan with butter when ready to serve. Heat the oil in a deep-fat fryer and fry the kale in small batches. Drain and season. (You can use samphire instead of the other seaweeds.)

To serve
Place the sole in the centre of the plate. Add some pommes noisettes to one side, the seaweed to the other and spoon over the sabayon.

County chef:
Nigel Haworth
Restaurant:
Northcote

In 1996, Northcote became the first restaurant in Lancashire to receive a Michelin star and has kept it ever since. Chef and co-owner Nigel Haworth is Lancashire born and bred and is hugely proud of his county's cooking and produce.

He was championing the use of local food 20 years ago, long before it became fashionable, and works with farmers to help them develop and perfect their products. Northcote has won many accolades, including being named one of the top ten restaurants outside London last year.

"Lancashire is a very varied county. There's the beautiful countryside of the Pennines, the big industrial towns, and the seaside. And there's Blackpool, the Las Vegas of the north. Who could ask for more? We just had to make Lancashire Hot Pot while we there, of course, and it's one of Dave's favourites. By heck, it was good.

We had some of the best duck we'd ever eaten while we were in Lancashire and went to see the supplier – Reg Johnson of Goosnargh Ducks. At one time, the London chefs used to get their ducks from France. Now they go to Reg for his birds, which are traditionally reared and hung for 48 hours to enhance their flavour. Colin Nelson claims that his Ormskirk new potatoes are the best you'll ever taste and we thought he was right. He reckons they should be eaten the day they are dug, so we went and dug our own the day of the cook-off – they went perfectly with our duck."

Lancashire

Lancashire Hotpot

For us, this is the ultimate in comfort food. We cooked it outside Blackburn Cathedral and added good black pudding and kidneys to make a rich and irresistible stew. Ecky thump lad, this is champion.

Serves 6–8

2 tbsp olive oil

1kg neck of lamb or good chump chops, boned and diced

4 lambs' kidneys, cored and trimmed into quarters

2 onions, sliced

½ tsp salt

1 tbsp plain flour

250ml lamb stock

1 tbsp Worcestershire sauce

1 sprig of thyme

2 bay leaves

1kg good old potatoes, peeled and sliced

2 black pudding rings, skinned and sliced

50g butter, cut into cubes, plus extra for greasing the dish

Warm the olive oil and brown the lamb and kidneys, then set aside. Using the same pan with the meat juices and residue, sweat the onions with half a teaspoon of salt for a couple of minutes to draw out the moisture. Add the flour and stir to coat the onions. Add the stock, Worcestershire sauce, thyme and bay leaves and stir to make a lovely thick gravy.

Preheat the oven to 180°C/Gas 4. Butter a lidded casserole dish, add a layer of potato slices on the bottom and season with salt and black pepper. Add half the lamb and kidney mixture. Then add about half the black pudding slices and pour in half the gravy. Cover with another layer of potato slices, season them, then add meat and black pudding as before and pour in the rest of the gravy. You might like to arrange the top layer of potato slices to make a scalloped pattern. Dot with butter cubes.

Cover with the lid and place in the oven for 20 minutes. Take the lid off and cook for another 20 minutes until the potatoes on the top are golden.

Nigel Haworth's Wood Pigeon Breasts and Confit Legs

with celeriac and salted hazelnuts

You'll need to plan ahead for this one, as the pigeon legs need to marinate for four hours and take a long time to cook.

Serves 2

Celeriac purée
200g celeriac
20g butter
200ml cream

Pigeon breasts and confit legs
2 wood pigeons, plucked and cleaned
1 tbsp butter
2 sprigs of thyme
1 garlic clove, crushed
20g salt rock
100ml sunflower oil
chopped chives
2 sheets of brick pastry
vegetable oil for deep frying

Celeriac velouté
500ml chicken stock
2 roasted pigeon carcasses
20g butter

Salted hazelnuts
30g sugar
2 tbsp water
30g hazelnuts, roasted and peeled
pinch of Maldon sea salt

Spinach
1 tbsp butter
200g spinach
nutmeg and salt to taste

To make the celeriac purée
Peel the celeriac and cut into small dice. Melt the butter in a heavy-bottomed pan, then add the celeriac. Season with salt and sweat for 2–3 minutes, but do not allow the celeriac to colour. Add the cream, cover and cook until the celeriac is tender. Once the celeriac is tender transfer it to a blender and blitz until smooth. Check the seasoning, pass the purée through a fine sieve and set aside.

To prepare the pigeon breasts
Wash and dry the pigeons and check that all the feathers have been removed. Using a sharp knife, remove the legs and wishbones and set them aside for cooking separately. Place each crown of pigeon into a vacuum bag and seal tight. Put the bags in a sous-vide water bath at 68°C for 24 minutes. (For information on this technique, see page 68.) Remove and leave to rest for 5–10 minutes, then take the pigeon crowns out of the bags and season with salt and black pepper.

Heat a small amount of oil in a frying pan, add the pigeon crowns and colour on both breasts. Add the butter and baste for 2–3 minutes. Place the crowns on to a board and remove the breasts.

To prepare the confit legs

Place the pigeon legs on a stainless steel tray and sprinkle with thyme and crushed garlic. Sprinkle on the salt, covering the pigeon legs well, then cover with clingfilm and leave in the fridge for 4 hours to marinate. Wash off the marinade under cold running water and dry the pigeon legs. Place the legs in a vacuum bag with 100ml of sunflower oil and seal, then cook them in a preheated water bath for 6 hours at 80°C. Remove and leave until cold, then carefully remove the legs from the bag and drain well. Take the meat off the bones and shred into pieces. Put the shredded meat into a bowl, add 1 tablespoon of the celeriac purée and chives and check the seasoning. Divide the mixture into 2 equal balls and chill.

Put a sheet of brick pastry through the tagliatelli roller of a pasta machine to make long strands of pastry. Brush the pastry with melted butter. Place a ball of confit pigeon at one end of a pastry strand and roll around the ball to make a nest around the meat. Repeat with the other ball of meat. Cook in vegetable oil at 180°C in a deep-fat fryer until golden and crisp. Drain on kitchen paper and season with salt.

To make the celeriac velouté

to serve:
Put 3 small spoonfuls of celeriac purée on each plate, then add 3 small spoonfuls of wilted spinach. Carefully place two pigeon breasts on the middle of the plate and add a pigeon leg parcel. Scatter around the hazelnuts and finish with a small amount of celeriac velouté sauce.

Pour the chicken stock into a large pan, bring to the boil and add the pigeon carcasses. Gently simmer until the stock is reduced by half. Remove the carcasses and pass the stock through a fine sieve. Pour it back into a clean pan and whisk in half the celeriac purée and the butter. Check the seasoning.

To prepare the salted hazelnuts

Put the sugar in a pan with 2 tablespoons of water until it reaches soft boil stage – check with a sugar thermometer. Add the roasted hazelnuts and carefully mix them into the sugar so it crystallises around them. Add the Maldon sea salt and mix well, then turn the nuts out on to a tray to cool.

To cook the spinach

Melt the butter in a hot pan, add the spinach and season with salt and nutmeg. Gently cook the spinach until just wilted. Place on kitchen paper and keep warm.

Goosnargh Duck Confit and Duck Breast
with spiced roasted plums and Lancashire black peas

To get the very best from a duck, the legs and thighs need to be cooked for a long time and the breast more briefly and left pink. Be brave and deconstruct your duck to get the best of both worlds. We used Ormskirk new potatoes when we cooked this and they were fab.

Serves 4

Duck confit
3 tbsp sea salt
4 duck legs with thighs
6 sprigs of thyme
1 bay leaf
1 star anise
4 garlic cloves, sliced
1 shallot
500ml duck fat

Seared duck breast with plums
4 duck breasts
5 tsp chopped thyme
3 tsp ground black pepper
1½ tsp sea salt
6 ripe purple plums, halved and pitted

1 tbsp olive oil
½ tsp sugar

Potatoes
500g baby new potatoes, washed
200g frozen peas
good knob of butter
1 small bunch of mint, finely chopped

Black peas
250g black peas prepared as packet
    (usually have to be soaked
    overnight and boiled for 3 hours)
50g butter
1 tsp finely chopped thyme

To make the duck confit
Start this 36 hours ahead of eating. Place 1 tablespoon of the salt in a casserole dish and lay the duck legs on top of it, skin-side up. Place the remaining salt in a pestle and mortar with the thyme, bay leaf, star anise and some black pepper and grind to a rough crumble. Scatter this mixture over the duck legs and top with the garlic and shallot slices. Cover with clingfilm and leave for 24 hours to 'salt'.

When the 24 hours is up, melt the duck fat in a saucepan and preheat the oven to 150°C/ Gas 2. Brush the spices and salt residue from the duck portions and discard. Pack the duck portions into a casserole dish and pour over the duck fat. Put in the oven for 3 hours. Remove, transfer the duck to a bowl and pour over the fat, then leave to cool. It will keep like this for ages.

To prepare the seared duck breast with plums

Score the duck breasts in a nice tidy criss-cross pattern, piercing the skin but not the meat. Mix 4 teaspoons of the chopped thyme with 2 teaspoons of black pepper and 1 teaspoon of salt. Sprinkle this evenly over both sides of the duck breasts and leave for a few minutes while the flavours infuse.

Preheat the oven to 190°C/Gas 5. Place the plums on a baking sheet and mix the remaining thyme, salt and black pepper with the olive oil and sugar and rub over the plums. Place in the hot oven for 4 minutes until the skin of the plums begins to wrinkle. Turn them over and put back in the oven for another 4 minutes. Remove and keep somewhere warm while you cook the duck breasts. Leave the oven on.

Heat a large ovenproof frying pan and put the duck breasts in, skin-side down. Cook until they are golden and crisp. Turn them over and put them into the hot oven, skin-side up, for 8 minutes. Remove and leave to rest for 5 minutes before slicing.

To cook the potatoes

Cook the potatoes until tender, then crush. Cook the peas, drain and mix with the crushed potatoes. Add the butter and finely chopped mint.

To cook the black peas

Once the peas have been soaked and cooked, heat a frying pan with the butter and the thyme. Add the cooked black peas and heat through.

to serve:

Carve the duck breast into neat slices. Place a spoonful of black peas on the plate, put the confit on top and add 3 or 4 slices of duck breast. Add some new potatoes and roasted plums.

County chef:
Sean Hope
Restaurant:
The Red Lion Inn

The Red Lion Inn is in the village of Stathern in the beautiful Vale of Belvoir. Sean and his team take full advantage of the great produce on their doorstep, including game from Belvoir Castle, eggs, chickens and fruit from local farms, and veg from their own garden.

The menu changes daily according to what's available. Sean and his team have won a number of awards, including Best Local Produce Menu in 2007.

Leicestershire

"Beef, pork pies, Stilton cheese – all great in Leicestershire. It was a Leicestershire man named Robert Bakewell who changed the way cattle were bred and started to breed for beef, not milk. His techniques led to the Leicestershire Longhorn cattle – we met some of these delightful creatures on Pat and John Stanley's farm. They've been rearing Longhorns for 29 years and have won many awards for their herd and great meat. Then we visited Tuxford & Tebbutt, one of the oldest Stilton cheese makers, who still make the cheese by traditional methods. The smell in their dairy is quite incredible – nearly takes your head off – but the cheese is wonderful stuff. Red Leicester is another cheese from this region and we learned that in the old days most dairies kept pigs to eat the whey. Then what did they do with the pigs? Made pork pies of course! Melton Mowbray's raised pies are one of the county's most popular products."

Melton Mowbray Pork Pie

Raised pies like this look impressive but are actually very easy to make, so have a go. Use good-quality meat, season well and your pie will be a triumph.

Makes 4 small pies

Filling
400g shoulder of pork, finely chopped
55g fatty belly of pork, minced
55g lean bacon finely chopped
½ tsp ground allspice
½ tsp freshly grated nutmeg
1 egg, beaten

Jelly
900g pork bones
2 pig's trotters

2 large carrots and 2 celery sticks
1 onion
1 bouquet garni (thyme, bay, parsley)
½ tbsp black peppercorns

Pastry
150g lard
50ml full-fat milk
50ml water
450g plain flour
½ tsp freshly ground black pepper

To make the pastry
This is best done the day before making the pie. Put the lard, milk and water into a small pan. Heat until the lard has melted and the mixture is warm. Sift the flour into a large bowl, season with the pepper and a pinch of salt and mix well. Mix the warm lard liquid into the flour and knead to form a ball. Leave to rest in the fridge.

To prepare the jelly
Put all the jelly ingredients into a large saucepan. Add just enough water to cover the bones. Slowly bring to the boil, then reduce to a simmer. Remove any scum that comes to the top and continue to simmer for 3 hours. Strain through a fine sieve, pour into a clean pan and reduce the stock until you have about 600ml.

To make the pie
Preheat the oven to 180°C/Gas 4. Put all the meat, spices and seasoning for the filling into a large bowl and mix together well with your hands. Take a pie dolly (or a small jam jar) and rub it in plain flour to stop the pastry sticking. Knead a piece of pastry into a circle about 3cm thick. Lay the dolly on the disk and press the pastry up the sides of the dolly, using your thumbs to create the case. Then gradually ease the pastry away from the sides and remove the dolly.

Roll some meat into a ball and carefully throw it into the pastry case – this helps to get rid of excess air. Brush the top edges of the pastry with beaten egg. Cut a smaller circle of pastry to fit the top of the pie, place it on and press the edges to seal them together well. Brush the top with beaten egg and bake for 45 minutes to 1 hour. Once cool, cut 2 small holes in the top and pour in the liquid jelly and then leave to cool before serving.

to serve:
Serve cold with good piccalilli or chutney.

Sean Hope's Pork Faggots Braised in Cider
with spring vegetables

All the produce for this dish was local – pork from Scalford, cider from the Thirsty Farmer in Little Dalby and veg from the Red Lion's own kitchen garden.

Serves 2

Pork faggots
250g pig's liver,
   cleaned and roughly chopped
250g pig's heart,
   cleaned and roughly chopped
250g pork mince
300g breadcrumbs
2 large shallots and 1 leek, peeled and
   finely chopped
1 large carrot, peeled and finely chopped
1 chilli, finely chopped
1 garlic clove
2 juniper berries
1 tsp ground allspice
vegetable oil
250ml cider
2 tbsp freshly chopped parsley
2 tbsp sherry vinegar
100g caul

Cider sauerkraut
250ml cider
100ml sherry or cider vinegar

¼ cinnamon stick
¼ white onion, finely sliced
1 small white cabbage, finely sliced
2 tbsp Leicestershire honey
pinch freshly chopped thyme

Sage and onion potato rosti
2 large Maris Piper potatoes, shredded
½ small white onion, finely sliced
1 garlic clove, finely chopped
1 tbsp finely chopped sage
2 tbsp Welland Valley rapeseed oil
knob of butter

Caramelised apples
3 Granny Smith apples
25g butter
75g caster sugar

For serving
6 rashers of streaky bacon, cooked
   until crispy
cooked asparagus spears and baby turnips

To cook the pork faggots
Put the liver, heart and mince in a bowl and mix with the breadcrumbs. Season and set aside. Put the vegetables and spices in a saucepan and sweat with a little vegetable oil. Add the cider and boil to reduce completely, then allow to cool. Add the chopped parsley and mix everything into the meat. Add the vinegar and season to taste.

Preheat the oven to 180°C/Gas 4. Roll the faggots into even-sized portions (2 per person) and wrap each one in caul. Seal the faggots in a frying pan or roasting tin until golden brown, then roast in the oven for 15–20 minutes.

To make the cider sauerkraut

to serve:

Place a spoonful of sauerkraut in the middle of each plate. Add 2 faggots on top of the sauerkraut with a wedge of rosti between them. Place two caramelised apple segments on top and scatter the baby turnips and asparagus spears over and around the dish. Finish off with a rasher of crispy bacon. Add a deep-fried sage leaf

Pour the cider and vinegar into a large pan, add the cinnamon and bring to the boil. Add the onion and cabbage, then cook for about 10 minutes until just done. Season to taste, add the honey and finish with the chopped thyme. Leave to steep for 15 minutes before serving.

To make the rosti

Mix the potatoes, onion, garlic and sage together well and season generously with salt and ground black pepper. Warm the oil in a frying pan and add the butter. When the butter starts to foam add the rosti mix to the pan and pat down to form a cake. Fry for 2–3 minutes or until golden brown. Turn over and fry for a couple more minutes. Turn out on to a chopping board, cut into equal portions.

To prepare the caramelised apples

Peel, core and quarter the apples. Melt the butter in the pan, add the sugar and sauté the

Beef and Stilton Pie
with celeriac mash and honey-roasted beetroot

Frozen puff pastry is very good, but we made our own for this dish. For a special occasion, do have a go at making the pastry. It's not that hard and the results really are worth it.

Serves 4

Rough puff pastry
250g plain flour
250g very cold butter,
    cut into small cubes
½ tsp salt
125ml ice-cold water

Pie filling
1kg braising steak
2 garlic cloves, crushed
1 small bunch of thyme
1 tbsp black peppercorns
400ml Leicestershire pale ale
2 tbsp seasoned plain flour
1 tbsp vegetable oil
knob of butter
100g chestnut button mushrooms
8 shallots, halved

500ml good beef stock
75g Stilton cheese, crumbled
butter
1 egg, beaten

Celeriac and mustard mash
350g celeriac
800g Maris Piper potatoes
good knob of butter
150ml double cream
1 dsrtsp coarse grain mustard

Honey-roasted beetroot
500g cooked beetroot (not vinegared)
2 tsp fresh thyme
2 tsp balsamic vinegar
2 tbsp olive oil
2 tbsp clear honey

To prepare the rough puff pastry

Put the flour in a mound on your work surface and make a well in the centre. Put the butter and salt in the well and work everything together with the fingertips of one hand, gradually drawing the flour into the centre with the other hand. When the cubes of butter have become small pieces and the dough is grainy, gradually add the iced water. Mix until it is all incorporated, but don't overwork the dough. Roll it into a ball, wrap in clingfilm and refrigerate for 20 minutes.

Flour the work surface and roll out the pastry into a 40 x 20cm rectangle. Fold it into 3 and give it a quarter turn. Roll the block of pastry into a 40 x 20cm rectangle as before and fold it into 3 and turn again. Wrap the block in clingfilm and refrigerate for 30 minutes. Repeat the process, rolling and folding as before to make a total of 4 turns. The pastry is now ready. Wrap it in clingfilm and refrigerate for at least 30 minutes before using.

To make the pie

Place the braising steak, garlic, thyme, peppercorns and ale into a bowl. Cover and leave to marinate overnight or for at least 2–3 hours. Remove the beef from the marinade, pat dry and toss in the seasoned flour. Strain the marinade and keep the liquid. Heat the oil and butter in a casserole and brown the meat. Don't crowd the pan or the meat will stew, not colour, so best to do this in batches. Once all the meat is browned set it aside. Brown the chestnut mushrooms and shallots in the same pan for about 5 minutes, then put the beef back in the casserole with the marinade liquid and beef stock. Cover and simmer gently for about 1½ hours or until the meat is tender. Alternatively, you can cook the meat in the oven at 160°C/Gas 3 for the same length of time.

Strain off half the cooking liquid from the casserole and set aside to use as additional gravy for the pies and when serving. While the filling is still hot, crumble in the Stilton and mix well until melted. Season to taste and leave to cool. Preheat the oven to 180°C/Gas 4. Butter your mini pie dishes generously and sprinkle the inside with flour. Using a slotted spoon, fill the pie dishes with the beef and Stilton mixture, pressing it down gently to give a full and generous pie. Add a little of the extra liquid to each pie.

On a floured surface, roll out the puff pastry to a thickness of about 2.5cm – this will give a lovely raised puffy top to your pie. Cut out circles of the pastry slightly bigger than the pie dishes. Brush the edges of the circles with the beaten egg and place on top of the pie dishes. Crimp and trim off any excess pastry, making sure the pies are well sealed. Make a small hole in the top of each one to allow the steam to escape and brush with the remaining egg.

Place in the preheated oven and cook for 20–25 minutes until the pastry is crisp and golden. While the pies are cooking, reduce the remaining gravy to intensify the flavours – if you fancy, you could add a teaspoon of redcurrant jelly. Add a knob of butter to give your gravy a shiny finish.

To cook the celeriac and mustard mash

Peel the celeriac and cut into even chunks. Put them in a pan of cold, salted water, bring to the boil and simmer for 20–30 minutes until tender. Drain and mash. Cut the potatoes into even-sized chunks, cook in the same way, drain and mash. Put both vegetables into one pan over a low heat and stir in the butter, cream and mustard. Season to taste with salt and white pepper.

to serve:
Serve your perfect pies with the mash and beetroot on the side and a jug of gravy.

To cook the honey-roasted beetroot

Preheat the oven to 220°C/Gas 7. Using a small melon baller or similar, scoop out balls of beetroot. Mix the thyme, vinegar, olive oil and honey in a bowl. Add the beetroot balls, coat them well and season. Tip everything into a high-sided baking dish and roast for 15 minutes until the beetroot is sticky and glazed.

County chef:
Colin McGurran
Restaurant:
Winteringham Fields

Colin McGurran is chef-patron at Winteringham Fields in the quiet village of Winteringham. He has run the restaurant for four years and in 2008 it came fourth in the Good Food Guide's list of the top 40 restaurants in the country. It was also voted Northern Restaurant of the Year in 2007. Using local produce is high on Colin's list of priorities. He rears his own lamb, chickens and eggs for use in the kitchen and has vegetables and herbs grown on a neighbouring farm.

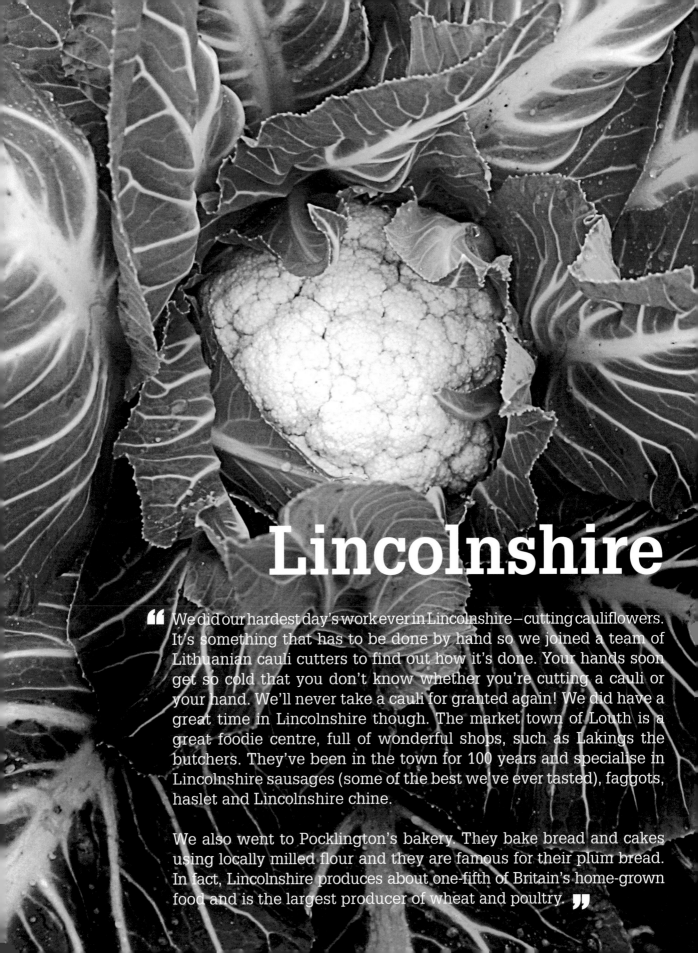

Lincolnshire

" We did our hardest day's work ever in Lincolnshire – cutting cauliflowers. It's something that has to be done by hand so we joined a team of Lithuanian cauli cutters to find out how it's done. Your hands soon get so cold that you don't know whether you're cutting a cauli or your hand. We'll never take a cauli for granted again! We did have a great time in Lincolnshire though. The market town of Louth is a great foodie centre, full of wonderful shops, such as Lakings the butchers. They've been in the town for 100 years and specialise in Lincolnshire sausages (some of the best we've ever tasted), faggots, haslet and Lincolnshire chine.

We also went to Pocklington's bakery. They bake bread and cakes using locally milled flour and they are famous for their plum bread. In fact, Lincolnshire produces about one-fifth of Britain's home-grown food and is the largest producer of wheat and poultry. "

Lincolnshire Plum Bread

There's good baking in Lincolnshire and this sweet plum bread is a traditional dish. Spread with butter, it's good to eat at breakfast time or for afternoon tea and works well with the local cheeses.

Serves 6–8

225g prunes, roughly chopped
50g currants
50g sultanas
150ml Earl Grey tea
450g strong plain flour
125ml milk
6 tbsp soft brown sugar

110g butter, melted
2 eggs, beaten
½ tsp vanilla extract
1½ tsp ground cinnamon
1½ tsp ground allspice
¼ tsp salt
15g dried yeast

Place the dried fruits in a bowl and pour in the Earl Grey tea. Mix well and leave to soak for 10 minutes.

Sift the flour into a large bowl. Pour the milk into a separate bowl, add the sugar, butter, eggs and vanilla extract, then whisk well to combine. Add the spices, salt and yeast, whisk once more, then pour on to the flour. Mix well to form a soft dough.

Strain the fruits, discarding the tea, and add them to the dough. Knead for 3–5 minutes until the dough is smooth and elastic. Put the dough into a clean bowl, cover with a tea towel and leave to rise until doubled in size – about 1–2 hours. Take the dough out and knead again lightly to knock out the air. Place in a large loaf tin and leave to rise for another hour.

Preheat the oven to 190°C/Gas 5. Bake the bread for 40–50 minutes until golden and risen. Allow to cool before slicing and serve with butter and cheese.

Colin McGurran's Lincolnshire Haslet Beignet
with rhubarb purée and sage foam

Lincolnshire haslet is a traditional pork meat loaf, which is seasoned with sage. Like the Lincolnshire sausages, it's a truly great product.

Serves 4

125g butter, cubed
150g plain flour
4 eggs
500g good-quality haslet from
  the butcher, diced into 1cm cubes
250g pork belly, cooked
1 shallot, finely chopped
30g sage leaves, cut into strips
30g tarragon leaves, cut into strips

oil for frying
4 rashers of streaky bacon

Rhubarb purée

200g rhubarb, trimmed and chopped
pinch of sugar and salt

Sage foam

250ml milk
110g sage leaves

To make the beignets

Bring 250ml of water to the boil in a pan, add the butter and stir until it melts. Add the flour all at once and, using a wooden spoon, beat it in continuously for 3 minutes. Leave to cool slightly. Add eggs one at a time, beating well until fully incorporated. Mix the haslet, pork belly, shallot and herbs together, then fold them into the beignet mix. Season well with salt and black pepper, then set aside to rest for 30 minutes. When you're ready to serve, heat the oil to 190°C in a deep-fat fryer. Spoon the mixture into balls and carefully place them into the hot oil and fry for 3 minutes. Remove and drain on kitchen paper.

To prepare the rhubarb purée

Put the rhubarb in a saucepan with a little water and cook over a medium heat until very soft. Drain and then blitz in a blender with a pinch of sugar and salt.

To make the sage foam

Boil the milk and take it off the heat as soon as it has boiled. Add the sage and blitz in a blender. Foam with a hand blender to create froth.

To cook the bacon

Preheat the oven to 180°C/Gas 4. Place a sheet of silicon paper on a heavy roasting tin and lay the bacon on it, stretching the rashers slightly. Place a sheet of parchment over the top and press flat with another baking tray. Cook in the oven until the bacon is crispy.

tip:

You can put anything into a beignet so it's worth a go and once you've got the knack, you've got it for life. You can make the beignet batter ahead of time and cook the beignets at the last minute.

to serve:

Place some rhubarb purée on each plate and add the haslet beignet in the middle. Add the sage foam and a rasher of crispy bacon.

Beef in Red Wine Herby Suet Pudding

with cauliflower cheese and kidneys cooked in sherry

This is basically a deconstructed steak and kidney pudding. Both braising and shin are good but give very different results – there is possibly more flavour in the shin but the braising steak is very, very tender. Do try the kidneys too. They're anything but offal – they're blooming great! Sautéed potatoes and some peas, cooked and crushed with a little butter, are good with this.

Serves 8

Beef in red wine

1 tbsp olive oil

50g fatty streaky bacon, finely chopped

2 tbsp plain flour

1kg braising steak or shin, trimmed carefully, and cut into 1cm cubes

2 onions, finely chopped

300ml red wine

500ml good beef stock

bouquet garni

(thyme, parsley and bay leaves)

2 tsp Worcestershire sauce

2 tsp brandy

Suet crust

375g self-raising flour

200g beef suet

1 tsp dried thyme

pinch of dried sage

1 tsp sea salt

110–150ml cold water

1 egg yolk

1 egg, beaten

Kidneys

2 tbsp olive oil

½ medium onion, finely diced

1 celery stick, finely diced

1 carrot, finely diced

2 garlic cloves, crushed

2 tsp fresh thyme leaves

8 lambs' kidneys, halved and cored

4 tbsp dry sherry (Manzanilla is good)

2 tbsp crème fraîche

2 tbsp finely chopped flat-leaf parsley

Cauliflower cheese purée

1 head of good Lincolnshire cauliflower, broken into florets

2 tbsp double cream

150g Lincolnshire Poacher cheese, grated

To prepare the beef in red wine

Heat the oil in a heavy-based pan and fry the bacon until it releases its fat. Season the flour with salt and pepper and roll the cubes of meat in the flour. Add them to the oil and bacon fat and brown. Add the onions and sweat for a few minutes, but do not let them brown. Pour in the wine and stock, then add the bouquet garni, Worcestershire sauce and brandy. Season carefully. Cover the pan and simmer for about 2 hours for braising steak, or 3 hours for shin. Once the meat is tender, turn up the heat and bring to the boil. Cook for about 30 minutes until the liquid has reduced to intensify the flavours. Remove from the heat and leave the beef to cool in the liquor.

To prepare the suet crust

Mix the flour, suet, thyme, sage and a pinch of salt, then add the water to make a firm dough. Knead in the egg yolk and put the dough in the fridge to chill – this will make it easier to roll out later.

To make the puddings

Roll out a ball of suet thinly to form a round. Using the end of a rolling pin, fold the dough over the edges to make a 'cup' shape. Place a buttered and floured pudding basin on top, then turn upright and remove the rolling pin.

Fill the suet case with meat and top with a little of the cooking liquid to keep the meat moist. Roll out a smaller ball to make the lid, brush the edges with the beaten egg and place on top. Use a rolling pin to roll around the top to seal and trim the edges. Repeat to make the rest of the puddings. Double-wrap them tightly with foil and steam them for about 30 minutes in a covered pan of water or a steamer. Unwrap them carefully and turn out of the moulds. Put any remaining meat and liquor into a pan and warm through. Strain into a clean pan, check the seasoning and finish with a knob of butter.

To prepare the kidneys

Heat the olive oil in a large frying pan and fry the onion, celery and carrot for about 5 minutes until the onion is translucent. Add the garlic and thyme, stir and cook for another minute. In a separate frying pan, add some olive oil and the kidneys and cook until just browned. Remove and add to the vegetables. Add the sherry to the pan in which the kidneys were cooked and deglaze. Pour this into the vegetables, cook for 1–2 minutes, then add the crème fraîche and warm through. Season and stir in the parsley.

To make the cauliflower cheese purée

Cook the cauliflower florets in boiling water until tender. Drain them in a colander, weighing them down with a plate to press out all the water – this recipe works better if the cauliflower is dry. Put the cauliflower in a food processor with the cream and whiz to make a fine purée. Season to taste, then return the mixture to a saucepan and stir through the cheese until it melts.

To serve

Cut a pudding in half and place one half upright and one half on its back. Spoon the kidneys alongside the pudding and add some cauliflower either side. Finish with a generous spoonful of sauce over the top.

The Hardwick is a country pub as well as a restaurant. Despite serious competition from restaurants such as the Walnut Tree, it was named Penderyn Restaurant of the Year in 2008 – this is the major award for restaurants in Wales. Stephen has worked with many of the greats in his career. His philosophy is to source the best local produce and treat it with the minimum of fuss to get the maximum flavour.

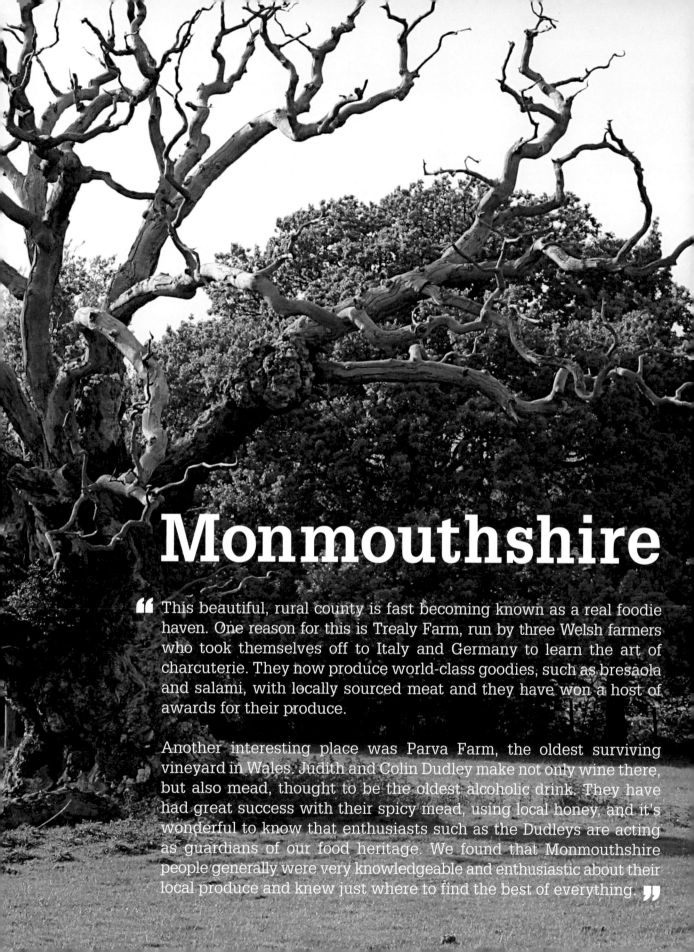

Monmouthshire

" This beautiful, rural county is fast becoming known as a real foodie haven. One reason for this is Trealy Farm, run by three Welsh farmers who took themselves off to Italy and Germany to learn the art of charcuterie. They now produce world-class goodies, such as bresaola and salami, with locally sourced meat and they have won a host of awards for their produce.

Another interesting place was Parva Farm, the oldest surviving vineyard in Wales. Judith and Colin Dudley make not only wine there, but also mead, thought to be the oldest alcoholic drink. They have had great success with their spicy mead, using local honey, and it's wonderful to know that enthusiasts such as the Dudleys are acting as guardians of our food heritage. We found that Monmouthshire people generally were very knowledgeable and enthusiastic about their local produce and knew just where to find the best of everything. "

Cawl

This is a Welsh stew – one of those dishes every family has their own recipe for. The ingredients traditionally depend on what is in season and what meat is available – mutton or bacon are the usual choices. It's best made the day before eating so the flavours have time to develop.

Serves 4

1kg Welsh neck of lamb, on the bone
cut into chunks
2 litres lamb stock
225g potatoes, peeled and diced
225g onions, peeled and sliced
225g leeks, sliced 1cm thick
225g carrots, peeled and sliced
225g swede, peeled and diced

Put the lamb into a large pan and pour over the stock. Bring to the boil and then turn down to simmer for a good hour. Add all the vegetables and continue to cook for another hour. Leave to cool.

The following day, reheat and bring back to the boil. Check the seasoning and cook for 15 minutes or until heated through. Serve with crusty bread and a good Welsh cheese.

Stephen Terry's
Old Spot Pork Belly
with lemon, broad beans and fennel

Pork and scallops work well together and this dish showed us that surf and turf can succeed in the hands of a master like Stephen.

Serves 8

Apple purée
4 Bramley apples
100g caster sugar
English mustard

Pork belly
½ large pork belly
1 ring of black pudding
20g flour
2 eggs, beaten
breadcrumbs
100ml rapeseed oil

Trimmings and garnish
12 king scallops
120g broad beans,
   podded and skinned
1 fennel bulb
3 unwaxed lemons,
   1 juiced and 2 cut into quarters
100ml extra virgin olive oil
   for dressing
rocket leaves

To make the apple purée
Peel, core and dice the apples. Put them into a saucepan over a medium heat, add the sugar and cook down to a purée. Leave to cool and then add English mustard to taste, about a dessertspoonful works well. Serve cold.

To cook the pork belly
Preheat the oven to 140°C/Gas 1. Place the pork in a roasting tray and half cover with water. Cover with a sheet of greaseproof paper, placing it directly on top of the belly, then put aluminium foil over the top of the roasting tray and fold down the edges to seal the pork in. Repeat this sealing process with a second sheet of foil. Place the pork in the oven and cook for 8 hours. Once the pork is cooked, carefully remove it from the cooking liquid and allow it to cool slightly on a tray, fat side up.

When the pork is cool enough to handle, the fun starts! Essentially, you need to deconstruct the belly and reconstruct it again, without all the bone, fat, skin and sinew. First, remove the skin from the belly and discard it. Reserve the soft underbelly fat. Remove all the pork belly meat and set it aside. Discard the bones and any extra fat and sinew. Mix the underbelly fat with the pork belly meat in a bowl – the fat will keep the belly moist when you reheat it to serve. Finely slice the black pudding ring.

Now you are ready to start reconstructing. You want the finished belly 'sandwich' to be approximately 4cm thick – about half the size of the original pork belly. Lay slices of black pudding on a baking tray, followed by a layer of pork belly meat. Repeat this process until you have used up all the meat. When you have finished layering the pork together, wrap it tightly in clingfilm and leave it to set in the fridge. Allow a minimum of 4 hours for this. When the meat is set, remove the clingfilm and cut into equal portions about 7cm x 3.5cm.

Preheat the oven to 160°C/Gas 3. Dip each portion in flour, egg and then the breadcrumbs. Shallow fry them in rapeseed oil over a medium heat until golden brown. Place the fried pork on a baking tray and put into the oven to heat through completely. This should take about 5 minutes.

To prepare the trimmings and garnish

While the pork is heating up, sear the scallops in a hot pan with a little oil for 1 minute on each side. Bring a saucepan of water to the boil and cook the broad beans for 2–3 minutes.

Slice the fennel finely, including the leafy top, and place the slices in some iced water to crisp. Just before serving, dress the fennel with the juice of a lemon and the olive oil.

to serve:

Cut each belly portion in half lengthways and place on a serving plate. Top with a small amount of the apple purée. Garnish with fennel and rocket. Place the scallops in between the belly portions on top of the fennel. Sprinkle broad beans around each belly and season with sea salt and freshly ground black pepper. Garnish with lemon wedges.

Smoked Roasted Pig's Cheeks
with pickled cabbage and mead and herb jelly

We found some amazing pork products in Monmouthshire – great cured ham, sausages and pancetta from Trealy Farm, as well as more unusual items, such as pig's cheeks, which is what we decided to try cooking. We like the idea of using the local mead in this dish as well.

Serves 4

Mead and herb jelly
3 gelatine leaves
250ml chicken stock
2 tbsp mead
1 tbsp dry white wine
1 tbsp very finely chopped thyme

1 medium head of cabbage
¼ tsp celery seeds
pinch of allspice
60g sugar
60ml white wine vinegar
100ml water

Pig's cheeks and pickled cabbage
2 smoked pig's cheeks

Pancetta garnish
8 thin rashers of pancetta

To make the jelly
Place the gelatine leaves in a bowl of cold water until they soften. Pour the chicken stock into a small pan and warm it through. Add the mead, wine and gelatine leaves and stir until the gelatine has dissolved, then add the chopped thyme. Pour on to a flat dish (so it is about 1cm deep) and leave to cool and set in the fridge. When the jelly is set, turn it out of the dish and cut into rough cubes – they can be quite rustic.

To cook the pig's cheeks and pickled cabbage
Preheat the oven to 180°C/Gas 4. Place the cheeks on a baking tray and roast for about an hour until golden.

Finely shred the cabbage. Put the celery seeds, allspice, sugar, vinegar and water into a medium saucepan, season with salt and pepper and bring to the boil. Add the shredded cabbage and cook for 10–15 minutes. Transfer to a bowl, cover with clingfilm and set aside so the flavours can infuse. While still warm, drain the cooking liquor and serve.

to serve:
Place some cabbage on each plate and add some sliced pig's cheek on top. Scatter the jelly cubes around the dish and decorate the plate with crispy pancetta garnish.

To prepare the pancetta garnish
Preheat the oven to 180°C/Gas 4. Place a sheet of silicon paper on a heavy roasting tin and lay out the pancetta on it. Place a sheet of parchment over the top and press flat with another baking tray. Place in the oven and cook until the pancetta is stiff and crispy.

County chef:
Chris Morrison
Restaurant:
Mansefield Hotel

Chris Morrison is a Moray man, born and bred, and hugely proud of his county and its food. The hotel is in the heart of Speyside, which is malt whisky country, and there are about 40 distilleries within 20 miles. Chris likes to cook both traditional Scottish dishes and modern British food and was named Speyside Chef of the Year in 2009. He has built up a close relationship with local farmers and butchers and likes to promote Moray produce in the restaurant.

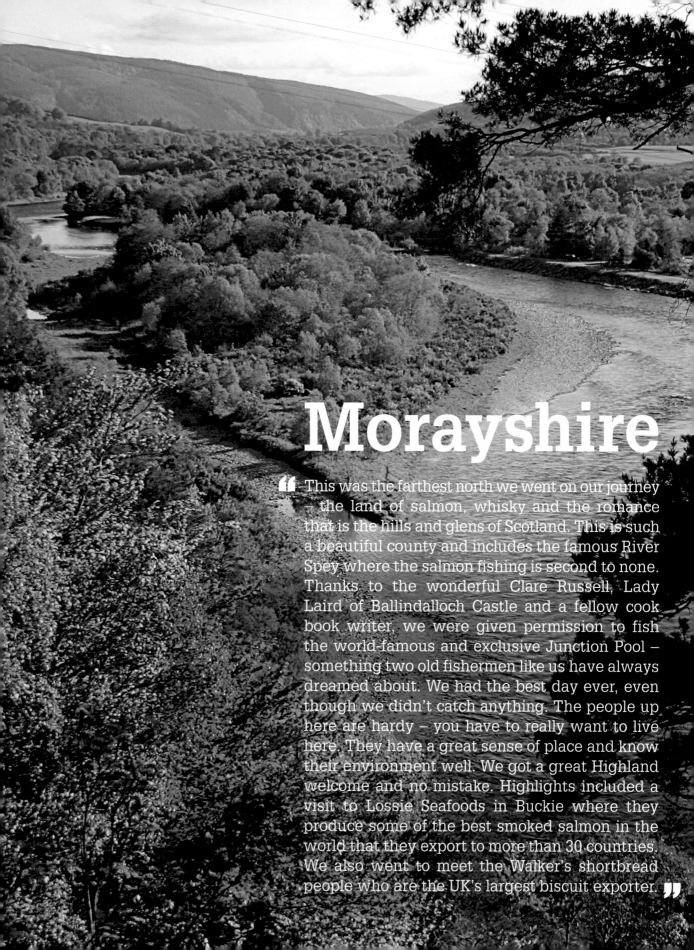

Morayshire

This was the farthest north we went on our journey – the land of salmon, whisky and the romance that is the hills and glens of Scotland. This is such a beautiful county and includes the famous River Spey where the salmon fishing is second to none. Thanks to the wonderful Clare Russell, Lady Laird of Ballindalloch Castle and a fellow cook book writer, we were given permission to fish the world-famous and exclusive Junction Pool – something two old fishermen like us have always dreamed about. We had the best day ever, even though we didn't catch anything. The people up here are hardy – you have to really want to live here. They have a great sense of place and know their environment well. We got a great Highland welcome and no mistake. Highlights included a visit to Lossie Seafoods in Buckie where they produce some of the best smoked salmon in the world that they export to more than 30 countries. We also went to meet the Walker's shortbread people who are the UK's largest biscuit exporter.

Cullen Skink

This traditional soup is named after the town of Cullen in Moray and is still popular with the locals.

Serves 4

Stock	**Soup**
75g butter	75g butter
vegetable oil	vegetable oil
2 leeks, roughly chopped	2 leeks, finely chopped
2 onions, roughly chopped	2 shallots, finely chopped
2 fennel bulbs, roughly chopped	2 garlic cloves, crushed
1 large glass of white wine	300g potatoes, peeled and diced
500g smoked haddock	500g smoked haddock
750ml water	500ml double cream
	1 tbsp finely chopped parsley
	freshly grated nutmeg

Start by making the stock. Heat the butter and a little oil in a pan, add the roughly chopped leeks, onions and fennel and sweat until soft. Pour in the white wine and bring to the boil, then add the haddock. Pour in the water, bring to the boil again, then simmer for 30 minutes, removing any scum from the top. Strain through muslin and set aside.

In another large saucepan, heat the other 75g of butter with a little vegetable oil and add the finely chopped leeks, shallots and garlic. Add the diced potatoes and haddock, then pour in the strained stock and bring to the boil. Simmer for 10–15 minutes until the potatoes are tender. Add the cream and, using a hand blender, carefully blitz so that you still have chunks of potato and fish in the soup but half of the liquid is puréed.

To serve
Serve with crusty bread and sprinkle with chopped parsley and nutmeg.

Chris Morrison's Grilled Halibut and Langoustines
with smoked haddock risotto and shellfish froth

This fish was spanking fresh, delivered that morning, and tasted wonderful. Always buy the best fish you can find – it'll be worth every penny.

Serves 4

4 x 300g halibut fillets
8 langoustine tails, shelled
olive oil
chervil to garnish

Shellfish froth
1 tbsp olive oil
50g butter
8 langoustine shells
1 onion, roughly chopped
1 carrot
1 fennel bulb
2 bay leaves

2 tbsp tomato purée
good splash of Glenlivet whisky
250ml cream

Smoked haddock risotto
1 onion, finely diced
2 tbsp olive oil
50g butter
250g arborio rice
about 500ml boiling water
100g shelled peas
250g smoked haddock fillets
4 tbsp freshly grated Parmesan

To make the shellfish froth
Heat the oil and butter in a pan. Add the langoustine shells, vegetables and bay leaves and sweat for 20 minutes. Add the tomato purée and cook for another 5 minutes. Deglaze the pan with the whisky and cook to reduce slightly. Add 1.2 litres of water, bring to the boil and simmer for 30 minutes. Strain the mixture through a fine sieve, then return to a gentle heat. Pour in the cream and season. Using a hand blender, blitz to make a froth.

To make the risotto
Sweat the onion in the olive oil and butter. Stir in the rice, coating it thoroughly in the butter and oil. Adding a ladleful of boiling water at a time, cook the rice until tender. Add the peas and smoked haddock and cook until the fish starts to fall apart. Check for seasoning and finish with a light sprinkle of Parmesan.

to serve:
Place a spoonful of risotto in the centre of each plate. Top with halibut and langoustine tails. Surround with a little shellfish froth and garnish with chervil.

To cook the halibut and langoustines
Season the halibut and langoustines with salt and pepper and drizzle them with a little olive oil. Heat a frying pan and add the halibut skin-side down. Cook for 30 seconds to 1 minute depending on the thickness of the fish, then turn over and cook on the other side. Remove from the heat and place the fish on a baking tray. Add the tails and finish under a preheated grill.

Wild Salmon on a Bed of Lentils
with smoked salmon Scotch eggs

Moray is famous for the quality of both its fresh wild salmon and its smoked salmon. We use both in this recipe. We also cooked some honey-roasted wild sea trout – what a garnish!

Serves 4

Lentils

350g green or puy lentils, washed
1 carrot, peeled and finely diced
1 celery stick, finely diced
1 garlic clove, crushed
1 small onion, peeled and finely diced
2 sprigs of thyme
50g butter

Salmon

4 pieces of wild salmon fillet, skin on
2 tsp chopped fresh tarragon
4 tsp chopped fresh parsley
2 tsp chopped chives
1 tsp sea salt flakes
½ tsp ground black pepper
1 tsp sugar
1 tsp lemon juice
zest of ½ lemon
1 tbsp olive oil
1 tbsp vegetable oil

Smoked salmon Scotch eggs

12 quails' eggs
1 shallot, finely chopped
250g smoked salmon
50g fresh breadcrumbs
1 tbsp chopped mixed herbs
(chervil, dill, parsley and chives)
1 tsp lemon juice
1 egg yolk
2 tbsp flour
1 egg, beaten
3 tbsp sesame seeds
vegetable oil for deep frying

Salad

rapeseed oil
lemon juice
baby salad leaves

To cook the lentils

Put the lentils in a pan with about 750ml of boiling water, cover and simmer for about 15 minutes. Add the carrot, celery, garlic, onion and thyme and simmer for another 15 minutes until tender. Season with salt and pepper and simmer for 5 minutes more.

Keep an eye on the lentils and don't let them dry out or get too mushy – either of which is a bad thing. Set aside, ready to warm up with the butter before serving.

To prepare the salmon

First, make 3 or 4 small cuts in the skin side of each piece of salmon and place thaem in a shallow dish. Mix the herbs, sea salt, pepper, sugar, lemon juice and zest and the olive oil in a separate bowl, then use this citrusy marinade to cover both sides of the salmon. Leave for about three-quarters of an hour for the flavours to infuse.

Preheat the oven to 180°C/Gas 4. Heat the vegetable oil in an ovenproof frying pan. Shake off the excess herbs from the salmon, then place the pieces in the pan, flesh-side down, and fry until golden. Turn over and sear the skin side for a couple of minutes.

Transfer the pan to the oven for about 10 minutes until the fish is cooked through.

To prepare the Scotch eggs

Boil the quails' eggs for 2 minutes, then plunge them into ice-cold water, peel and set aside. Sweat the shallot in a little oil until soft. Then put the smoked salmon, shallot, breadcrumbs, fresh herbs, lemon juice and egg yolk in a blender or food processor, with some seasoning, and process to a paste.

Take a knob of the salmon mixture and shape it around a quail's egg so the egg is evenly covered. Repeat to coat all the eggs. Roll them in flour, then dip in the beaten egg. Lastly, press the eggs into the sesame seeds and then put them in the fridge until ready to fry.

When you're ready to eat, heat some oil in a pan for deep-frying. When it's hot, drop in the Scotch eggs and fry for a moment or two until the seeds are golden. Taken them out and drain on kitchen paper.

To prepare the salad

Dead simple this bit. Make the dressing with rapeseed oil and lemon juice, then drizzle it on to the greenery.

To serve

Place a bed of lentils on each plate and add a piece of salmon on top. Add a few of the little Scotch eggs and some salad leaves alongside them.

County chef:
Galton Blackiston
Restaurant:
Morston Hall

Galton is chef-proprietor of Morston Hall, near Blakeney, which is one of the best restaurants in the county and has a Michelin star and three AA rosettes. Galton knows he is lucky to have such great ingredients on his doorstep, a steady stream of local producers arrive at his kitchen every day, bringing such delights as Blakeney lobsters, Morston mussels, Norfolk apples and wild mushrooms.

Norfolk

"Norfolk has a very rural, slightly old-fashioned feel in the nicest possible way. The coastline is glorious and well known for the many foodie goodies it supplies, such as samphire and the most succulent crabs. We went out on a crabbing boat from Cromer and collected about 80 crabs from 120 pots. The Cromer crabs are small but very sweet and meaty – we couldn't wait to eat them. Samphire is another Norfolk favourite and grows on the marshes along the coast. We went gathering samphire with Peter, the owner of the wonderful Cookie's Crab Shop in Diss, and learned that it makes the perfect accompaniment to crab.

Then we went to Great Snoring Farm – love the name! – to meet David Perowne who is the fifth generation of his family to work on the farm. He rears hens, ducks, quail and geese for eggs and has around 30,000 free-range birds. We bought some duck eggs – spanking fresh they were – for our cook-off dish (see page 182)."

Norfolk Dumplings
with mince and boiled potatoes

When we did our mobile kitchen in Diss we got involved in the Great Norfolk Dumpling War. Some people insisted that a Norfolk dumpling must contain suet. Others said no suet, just flour. We decided to go with the no-suet camp, but if you do want to include suet, use two parts flour to one part suet and you'll be happy.

Serves 12

Mince
3 tbsp olive oil
3 onions, finely diced
2½ organic beef stock cubes
2kg beef mince
1 tbsp Worcestershire sauce
2 tbsp gravy browning powder

Dumplings and vegetables
1.5kg self-raising flour
6 tbsp finely chopped parsley
500–750ml cold water
3kg white potatoes, peeled and chopped
150g butter
600g young carrots, scrubbed, topped and tailed

tip:
Don't let on in Diss, but we think that dumplings are best made with suet.

To prepare the mince
Heat a large casserole dish, add the oil and onions and cook for 3–4 minutes until the onions are softened. Add the stock cubes and cook for 1 minute before adding the mince. Fry the mince until it is just browned, then add the Worcestershire sauce and a litre of water and bring to a simmer. Add the gravy browning powder, a little salt and black pepper and simmer for 3 hours, stirring occasionally. Season once more with salt and black pepper.

To prepare the dumplings and vegetables
Mix the flour and parsley together in a bowl and season with salt and black pepper. Gradually add the water until the mixture forms a firm dough. Knead briefly until smooth, then roll into small pieces about the size of a golf ball.

Put the potatoes in a pan of salted water and bring to the boil. Add the dumplings carefully, then cover and return to a simmer. Cook for 15 minutes until the dumplings have risen and the potatoes are cooked through. Take the dumplings out of the pan before draining the potatoes and adding half the butter to the potatoes. Rest the dumplings on kitchen paper to absorb any excess moisture.

Bring a pan of salted water to the boil, add the carrots and cook for 4–5 minutes until tender. Drain and season with the remaining butter, salt and black pepper.

To serve
Spoon the dumplings on to the plates. Top with a spoonful of mince, then place some potatoes and carrots alongside it.

Galton Blackiston's Sea Trout

with carrots, asparagus and butter sauce

Using clingfilm to keep the trout fillets in shape is a great tip here and doesn't cause any problems as long as the pan isn't searingly hot and the clingfilm doesn't come into direct contact with the pan.

Serves 4

1 x wild sea trout, filleted, skinned and trimmed
450g cockles
110g butter
12 small young carrots, scrubbed, topped and tailed
12 asparagus spears, peeled and trimmed
1 tbsp olive oil
400g cooked new potatoes, sliced
75g samphire

Butter sauce
1 shallot, peeled and
  finely chopped
1 tbsp white wine vinegar
1 tbsp white wine
1 tbsp lemon juice
175g salted butter
3 tbsp chopped chives

To prepare the sea trout

Place the 2 trout fillets on top of each other. Roll them in clingfilm to form a long log, then wrap tightly with a little more clingfilm. Twist the ends in opposite directions to make the shape even tighter. Place in the fridge for at least 1 hour to firm up.

Heat a large sauté pan, add the cockles and a glass of water, cover and cook for 2–4 minutes until all the cockles have opened. Drain and remove the cockles from their shells, discarding any that haven't opened. Set the cockle meat aside, discarding the liquid.

to serve:

Remove the clingfilm from the outside of the trout. Pile 3 carrots to one side of the plate and top with 3 stems of asparagus. Pile some potatoes into the centre of the plate. Top with 3 slices of the sea trout and spoon the butter sauce over the top and around.

Cut the sea trout into 12 thick slices – leaving the clingfilm on. Warm a frying pan, add a little of the butter and fry the sea trout slices on each side for 1 minute, then remove from the pan and rest. Bring 2 pans of salted water to the boil, put the carrots in one and the asparagus in the other and cook until tender. Drain the asparagus and carrots and toss with a little of the butter, salt and black pepper. Heat a frying pan, add the remaining butter, oil and new potatoes and fry until golden and just crispy. Add the samphire, toss through and cook for 1–2 minutes longer, then season with salt and black pepper.

To make the butter sauce

Place the shallot, white wine vinegar, white wine and lemon juice into a saucepan and bring to the boil. Cook until the liquid has reduced down to just 1 tablespoon Gradually whisk in the butter, a little at a time. When all the butter has been added, remove from the heat, add the cooked cockles and chives, and season with salt and black pepper.

Warm Potted Cromer Crab
with Norfolk samphire in caper sauce, poached duck egg and crab cakes

Crab is best served simply and there is nothing better than warm potted crab dressed with hot butter and light spices as here. The little crab cakes are delicious too – always use the brown meat as well as the white in crab cakes.

Serves 4

Potted crab
2 or 3 dressed crabs
250g unsalted butter
1 small shallot, finely chopped
pinch of mace and cayenne pepper
½ tsp nutmeg
1 tsp lemon juice
zest of ½ lemon
1 pack of micro cress

Samphire
250g samphire (a good handful)
4 tbsp white wine
75g unsalted butter
1 tbsp extra-small capers, rinsed
1 tbsp finely chopped parsley

Duck eggs on toast
splash of white wine vinegar
4 duck eggs
4 slices of good bread
50g butter

Crab cakes
1 dressed crab
1 tbsp finely chopped fresh parsley
½ tsp English mustard
½ tsp Worcestershire sauce
1 duck egg yolk, beaten
1 tbsp crème fraîche
1 tsp lemon juice
zest of ½ lemon
2–3 tbsp breadcrumbs, made from stale white bread, plus extra for coating
2 tbsp flour
1 duck egg, beaten
2 tbsp vegetable oil for frying

Lemon mayonnaise
3 duck egg yolks
1 tbsp Dijon-type mustard
1 tbsp lemon juice
400ml rapeseed oil

tip:
We have a great tip for poaching eggs. Before you crack the egg, just put it in the boiling water in its shell for 20 seconds. Makes the white that bit firmer.

To prepare the potted crab
Separate the white and brown crab meat and set aside. Heat the butter in a pan until it foams, then pass it through a strainer. You will be left with the scum in the sieve and clarified butter in the bowl. Put the clarified butter in a pan and add the shallot, mace, cayenne pepper, nutmeg, lemon juice and zest. Bring this to a very slow simmer and leave to infuse for 15 minutes. Remove from the heat and sieve again. Pour this spiced clarified butter on to the white crab meat and mix in well.

Preheat the oven to 150°C/Gas 2. Grease 4 small dariole moulds and line them with clingfilm. Half fill each mould with white crab meat, pressing it down well. Spoon on a layer of brown crab meat and press down. Finish with another layer of the white crab meat, again pressing down well. Cover each mould with clingfilm, then place them in a roasting tin. Pour in boiling water until it is halfway up the sides of the moulds, place in the oven and cook for 15 minutes. Remove and allow to cool slightly before peeling off the clingfilm and turning out the potted crab.

To prepare the samphire

Bring a pan of lightly salted water to the boil, then add the samphire and cook for 2–3 minutes. Drain and refresh in iced water. Heat the wine and reduce for a couple of minutes. Carefully whisk in the butter, then add the samphire, capers and parsley, then season and warm through.

To poach the duck eggs

Everyone has their own ideas about the perfect poached egg – here are ours. The most important thing is to use good fresh eggs. Take a frying pan, preferably one with deep straight sides, and fill it two-thirds full with water. Bring the water to the boil and add the vinegar – not too much or it will taste. Crack an egg on to a saucer, whisk the water around and slide the egg into the water. With a big spoon wrap the white around the yolk so it's nice and tidy and cook for about 4 minutes. Remove with a slotted spoon and plunge into iced water. Dry on kitchen paper and set aside. while you cook the rest. When ready to serve, plunge the poached eggs into boiling water for 30 seconds. Cut 4 rounds of bread with a pastry cutter, toast them and spread with butter.

To make the crab cakes

Mix together the crab meat, parsley, mustard, Worcestershire sauce, beaten egg yolk, crème fraîche, lemon juice and zest. Take care not to break up the crab too much. Add the breadcrumbs (adding a little more if necessary to make a thick paste) and mix well. Season to taste. Shape into small, flattened, walnut-sized cakes. Dust with flour, dip in beaten egg and coat with breadcrumbs. Place the crab cakes on a baking tray lined with silicon paper and chill in the fridge for half an hour. Heat the oil in a frying pan, add the crab cakes and fry on each side until golden and hot.

To make the mayonnaise

Whisk the egg yolks in a bowl and whisk in the mustard and lemon juice. Slowly start to add the oil while continuing to whisk – a little electric hand whisk will be fine for this – until the mixture thickens into lovely lemon mayonnaise. Season with salt and black pepper.

to serve:

Place the potted crab on the plate. Add the toast to one side and top with a poached egg. Pile the samphire to the other side and set 3 crab cakes on top. Spoon the sauce from the samphire pan around the plate. Finish with a few small blobs of mayonnaise around the edge and a sprinkling of micro cress.

County chef:
Emily Watkins
Restaurant:
Kingham Plough

Emily Watkins trained with Heston Blumenthal and worked as his number two at the Fat Duck. She now runs the Kingham Plough, a traditional country pub with great food in the north of Oxfordshire. The menu is simple and unfussy with some traditional dishes as well as more adventurous creations. Emily has a strict buy-local policy and reckons that 85 per cent of her suppliers are within 10 miles of the pub. She likes to use wild food too, and picks berries from the nearby hedgerows.

With its beautiful countryside and the gentle aura of academia, Oxfordshire is quintessentially English. There are historic towns, such as Oxford, Cirencester and Chipping Norton, but nestled amid the Cotswolds are also perfect little villages of honey–coloured houses. And, we discovered, there's good food as well as beauty.

We went to Foxbury Farm where they rear excellent beef, lamb and pork and also act as an outlet for other local producers. We took away some great stuff for our Oxford sausages. Another treat was visiting Alex James, guitarist with Blur, who has created his own cheese with neighbour and cheese expert Juliet Harbutt. Their Little Wallop goat cheese is quite something – and Si got to play drums with Alex! We love quince so we were interested to meet Elspeth and Colin Wainwright who decided to bring this fruit back on to the food map. They grow their own quince and make fantastic jelly, mustard and chutney.

Oxfordshire

Oxford Sausage Breakfast

The Oxford sausage isn't really a sausage at all, as it's naked and shaped like a letter C, but it's good. These are usually made with half pork and half lamb or veal and bulked out with suet. Makes a great breakfast.

Serves 4

Sausages

500g minced pork
500g minced lamb
350g shredded suet
225g fresh breadcrumbs
zest of 2 lemons
1 tbsp chopped rosemary leaves
1 tbsp chopped sage leaves
1 tsp freshly grated nutmeg
salt and black pepper
1 egg, beaten
a little flour for coating
50g goose fat, butter or oil for frying

Breakfast

8 slices of middle-cut smoked bacon
4 tomatoes, halved
1 loaf white or brown bread, thickly sliced
110g butter
8 large Portobello mushrooms, peeled
2 tbsp vegetable oil
4 eggs

To make the sausages

Place the minced meats, suet, breadcrumbs, lemon zest, herbs, nutmeg and seasoning into a large bowl and mix well. Add the egg and mix again. Flour a chopping board and your hands, then take a small ball of mixture and roll into a sausage shape. Coat each sausage with a little flour then shape into a C.

Heat a frying pan and add the goose fat, butter or oil. Cook the sausages, a few at a time, over a gentle heat for 6–8 minutes until golden brown and cooked through.

To prepare breakfast

Preheat the grill to high and cook the bacon and tomatoes for 3–4 minutes on each side until cooked through. Keep them warm in the oven while you toast the bread. Meanwhile, heat a frying pan, add a quarter of the butter and cook the mushrooms for 2–3 minutes on each side until golden and tender. Heat a separate pan, add the oil and fry the eggs to your liking.

To serve

Pile the sausages, bacon, tomatoes, mushrooms and an egg on to each plate. Serve with the toast, remaining butter and a choice of Oxfordshire marmalade or honey.

Emily Watkins's Partridge
with violet dumplings

Emily is interested in trying different techniques, such as using a sous-vide to bring out the true flavour of food. For more information on this, see page 68.

Serves 4

Partridge
2 partridges, cleaned
110g goose fat
8 sage leaves
6 tbsp olive oil
400ml strong chicken stock
200g chicken hearts, cleaned and trimmed
2 sprigs of thyme

75g clarified butter
½ head savoy cabbage, finely sliced

Dumplings
750g violet potatoes, scrubbed
2 egg whites
50g semolina

To prepare the partridge
Remove the breasts and legs from the partridge and set the carcass aside. Place the legs in a vacuum bag with the goose fat. Seal, place into a water bath set at 64°C and poach for 4–6 hours. Take the legs out, remove the bones and set aside. Place the breasts into a vacuum bag with half the sage leaves and 4 tablespoons of the olive oil. Seal, place in a water bath set at 57°C and cook for 30 minutes. Another way of cooking the meat would be to wrap the legs in foil and roast in a low oven for several hours, and pan-fry the breasts.

Preheat the oven to 200°C/Gas 6. Roast the carcass for 20 minutes until browned. Take it out and place in a saucepan with the chicken stock. Bring to the boil, then reduce and simmer for 25–30 minutes until the liquid is thickened and reduced by half. Strain and set aside. Marinate the chicken hearts with the remaining olive oil, the rest of the sage leaves and the thyme.

When you're nearly ready to serve, heat a frying pan, add a little of the clarified butter and the cabbage and sauté for 3–4 minutes until tender. Heat another frying pan, add some clarified butter and the partridge breasts, skin-side down, and fry them for 2 minutes until crispy and heated through.

to serve:
Pile some cabbage into the centre of each plate. Spoon the dumplings and hearts around the edge and place the breasts on top of the cabbage. Reheat the sauce if necessary and spoon it around.

To make dumplings
Place the potatoes in a pan of water, bring to the boil and simmer for 1 hour until tender. Drain and peel while still warm, then immediately pass through a potato ricer into a bowl. Whisk the egg whites lightly, then add to the potatoes and mix well to make a firm dough. If possible, leave the mixture in the fridge to rest overnight. Dust the dough with semolina and roll out into a 2.5cm log. Cut the log into 2.5cm-thick diagonal slices.

Heat a frying pan, add the rest of the clarified butter and the dumplings and cook them for 2 minutes until golden. Add the chicken hearts and cook until caramelised. Then add the reduced chicken stock and heat for 1 minute. Add the partridge legs to warm through.

Loin of Kid and Quince Jelly Glaze
with goat's cheese dauphinoise potatoes, cumin carrot purée and buttered broad beans

Kid can be tough, but if properly hung before cooking, it is a delicious, healthy meat. Our quince jelly went perfectly with the meat and we do recommend the goat's cheese dauphinoise – a good twist on a classic.

Serves 4

Kid
12 rashers of smoked streaky bacon, halved
2 loins of kid, cut into 12 pieces about
   5cm thick
sunflower oil and a knob of butter for frying
leaves from 1 bunch of sage
50g quince and fig cheese, thinly sliced

Goat's cheese dauphinoise
50g butter
1.5kg waxy potatoes, thinly sliced
200g goat's cheese
2 garlic cloves, finely sliced
300ml double cream
300ml goat's milk

Quince jelly glaze
50g unsalted butter
1 garlic clove, crushed
150g quince jelly
1 tbsp chopped rosemary leaves
3 tbsp fresh beef stock

Vegetables
400g carrots, cut into small pieces
2 tbsp cumin seeds
200g broad beans (podded weight)
50g butter

To prepare the kid
Preheat the oven to 200°C/Gas 6. Stretch out the rashers of bacon, wrap a rasher around each piece of kid and secure it with a cocktail stick. Heat a frying pan, add the butter and oil and fry the pieces of kid on each side until browned. Put them on a roasting tray and cook in the preheated oven for 5–8 minutes, until the meat is just cooked and the bacon is crispy. Leave to rest for 5 minutes. Add a little more oil to the pan, and fry the sage leaves for 1 minute until crispy, then drain on kitchen paper.

tip:
Carrot and cumin go very well together so don't be nervous about trying this. It's important to blanch the seeds with the carrots so they are soft.

To make the quince jelly glaze
Heat a pan, add the butter and garlic and sweat for a couple of minutes without colouring. Add the quince jelly and stir until it has melted. Then add the rosemary and beef stock, season with salt and black pepper and cook gently for a couple of minutes.

To make the goat's cheese dauphinoise

Preheat the oven to 180°C/Gas 4. Butter a baking dish liberally – don't be shy. Carefully arrange the potatoes in layers, seasoning between the layers. When you have used about half the potatoes, crumble in the goat's cheese and garlic, then continue to layer the potatoes. Pour in the cream and goat's milk to cover the potatoes. Cover the dish with foil and place in the oven for about 1 hour. Remove the foil and return the potatoes to the oven for a further 15 minutes to crisp and colour the top. Cut into squares to serve.

To cook the vegetables

Bring a pan of salted water to the boil, add the carrots and cumin seeds and cook for 6–8 minutes until tender. Drain and blitz to a purée in a blender – adding a little cooking water if necessary. Season with salt and black pepper.

Bring a separate pan of salted water to the boil, drop in the broad beans and cook for 1–2 minutes. Drain them, refresh in cold water, then peel off the outer pale green shells of the beans. Put the beans back into a saucepan with the butter and warm through. Season with salt and black pepper.

to serve:

Place a square of potato on each plate and spoon on some quince jelly glaze next to the potato. Place 3 pieces of kid on to the glaze, then top with a slice of quince cheese and a deep fried sage leaf. Add some carrot purée and buttered broad beans.

County chef:
Will Holland
Restaurant:
La Bécasse

Will Holland is head chef at La Bécasse in the town of Ludlow. The restaurant opened in July 2007 and is owned by Ian Murchison, who also owns the Michelin-starred L'Ortolan in Berkshire.

La Bécasse won a Michelin star in January 2009 and also has three AA Rosettes. Will likes to use local produce whenever possible, but it must be of consistently good quality. He also enjoys combining local produce, such as pigeon, with more exotic ingredients like foie gras. He wants people to enjoy visiting La Bécasse and believes that fine dining should not be an exclusive, pretentious or intimidating experience.

Shropshire

"Shropshire is a foodie Mecca, packed with great independent shops, specialist food producers, fantastic restaurants – and greedy people like us! We loved it. Some of the treats we enjoyed were Ludlow sausages from one of the town's six butcher's shops, locally made beer and cider, and Shropshire blue cheese. Shropshire is also well known for its game and we went to visit a gamekeeper to find out how important partridge, pheasant and other game are to the local food scene. And we even went on a shoot. Guns are not really our sort of thing – we wanted to run for cover – but we went out on a perfect, crisp winter's day and had a great time. Game really does tick all the boxes, being sustainable, free-range and organic. What more could you ask? Then we went gathering wild fruit and berries with jam maker Sarah Jane Brough. She's a lovely lady and we met her in a bush! Sarah Jane makes the best preserves from fruits such as crab apples and wild blackberries and sells them at farmers' markets. Her hedgerow jam was just what we needed to go with the stuffed pheasant we cooked in Ludlow. "

Fidget Pie

This is a great traditional recipe that some locals had heard of and others hadn't. But they were all really excited about trying it. The combination of ham, Bramley apples and cider is just right.

Serves 8–10

500g shortcrust pastry

3 tbsp semolina

450g potatoes, peeled and thickly sliced

2 tbsp plain flour

110ml double cream

300g Bramley cooking apples,
    peeled and thickly sliced

2 onions, finely sliced

300g ham, thickly sliced

2–3 tbsp soft brown sugar

8 sprigs of sage, leaves chopped

110ml dry cider

1 egg, beaten

To prepare the pastry case

Preheat the oven to 190°C/Gas 5. Roll out two-thirds of the pastry to a thickness of about 5mm and use this to line a 23cm springform cake tin. Let the pastry hang over the edges of the tin to allow for shrinkage. Cover with a piece of baking parchment and fill with some baking beans or rice to stop the pastry rising while cooking.

Place the tin in the oven for 15 minutes, then remove the baking parchment and beans or rice and return to the oven for another 5–8 minutes to brown the base of the pastry. Remove, cool slightly then trim off any excess pastry. Sprinkle the semolina over the pastry to absorb any excess moisture in the filling.

To make the pie

Bring a pan of salted water to the boil, add the potatoes and simmer for 3–4 minutes until they are just tender. Drain and toss them with the flour, double cream, salt and black pepper.

Layer the filling ingredients into the base. Start with a layer of apples followed by potatoes, onions and ham and season as you go with sugar, sage, salt and black pepper. Add the cider, pouring it carefully so that it doesn't fizz up.

tip:

Do sprinkle the semolina over the pastry before adding the filling. It really does soak up the moisture and avoids soggy bottom syndrome!

Roll the remaining pastry into a disc that is big enough to cover the top of the pie. Brush the edges of the case with beaten egg and add the lid, pinching the pastry to form a seal around the edges. Place the pie in the oven for 1 hour until the pastry is golden brown and the filling is cooked through. Remove, and allow to cool slightly before serving in wedges with a pint of beer.

Will Holland's Roast Venison
with bitter chocolate, blackberries and beetroot

Wrapping the venison in streaky bacon helps keep it lovely and moist, but Will also basted it with plenty of melted butter.

Serves 4

Venison
1 long saddle of Mortimer Forest venison
6–12 slices of smoked streaky bacon
50g butter

Red wine marinade
1 carrot and 1 onion, chopped
1 head garlic, roughly chopped
1 sprig of thyme
1 celery stick, roughly chopped
1 leek, roughly chopped
12 black peppercorns
12 cloves
12 juniper berries
750ml red wine

Beetroot
6 large beetroot, peeled
5 litres water
1 sprig of thyme
1 bulb of garlic
750ml red wine vinegar
5 bay leaves
5g black peppercorns
375g sugar
100g salt

Salsify
6 salsify
1 litre brown chicken stock
1 sprig of thyme
3 garlic cloves
6 black peppercorns
3 bay leaves
salt and sugar to taste

75g sugar
1 litre beetroot cooking liquor

Poached blackberries
110g caster sugar
110g water
150g blackberries

Blackberry purée
500g blackberries
150g caster sugar
juice of ½ lemon,
500g beetroot trimmings

Braised red cabbage
zest and juice of 1 orange
5g black peppercorns
5g cloves and 5g star anise
1 cinnamon stick
100g demerara sugar
200g redcurrant jelly
50ml red wine vinegar
375ml red wine
1 large red cabbage, shredded

Salted grué de cacao tuiles
300g caster sugar
100g glucose
250g butter
100ml milk
5g pectin
300g grué de cacao
5g sea salt crystals

Sauce
100g butter
500g venison bones, chopped
50g carrot and onion, chopped
12 juniper berries
2 sprigs of thyme
2 bay leaves
500ml red wine marinade
(from reserved venison marinade)
1 litre brown chicken stock
50g bitter chocolate (70%
cocoa solids), finely grated
50ml crème de mûre

To prepare the venison Ask your butcher to remove the long strap loins and trim off all excess sinew. Also ask for the carcass to be chopped up as you'll need it for the sauce. Put all the red wine marinade ingredients into a bowl and mix them together. Add the venison loin and marinate for 1 hour, then take it out and pat dry with kitchen paper. Keep the marinade. Wrap the venison in thinly sliced smoked streaky bacon and cook it gently in a frying pan with the butter for about 12 minutes. Leave to rest before carving.

To prepare the beetroot and salsify Put the beetroot into a large pan with all the other ingredients in the beetroot list. Bring to a simmer and gently poach until tender – about 1 hour. Drain, keeping the cooking liquid. Using a melon baller, scoop the beetroot into small balls or cut into cubes. Keep the trimmings. Peel the salsify, putting them into acidulated water as you work to stop them going brown. Then put the salsify into a pan with all the ingredients in the salsify list and bring to a simmer. Gently poach for 12–15 minutes until tender. For the finishing liquor, pour 1 litre of the beetroot cooking liquid into a pan and bring to a simmer. Add the beetroot balls and salsify to heat through and glaze before serving.

To poach the blackberries Put the sugar and water into a saucepan and simmer until the sugar has dissolved. Add the blackberries and cook for 2–3 minutes until soft and warm.

To prepare the blackberry purée Put the blackberries in a pan with the sugar and lemon juice and cook them until they are soft and tender. Transfer them to a food processor, add the cooked beetroot trimmings and process until smooth. Pass the mixture through a fine sieve and set aside.

To prepare the red cabbage Put all the ingredients for the cabbage in a saucepan and bring to the boil. Reduce the heat and simmer gently for 2–3 hours or until the cabbage is soft and the liquor is reduced.

To prepare the tuiles Preheat the oven to 175°C/Gas 3½. Put the sugar, glucose, butter and milk in a saucepan and bring to the boil. Add the pectin and heat to 102°C on a sugar thermometer. Pour on to the grué de cacao and salt and mix well. Roll the mix thinly between 2 pieces of silicone paper and place on a baking sheet. Bake in the oven for 10–12 minutes or until crisp, then break into rough pieces.

To make the sauce Heat a sauté pan, add the butter and bones and caramelise until the bones are golden. Add the carrot, onion, juniper, thyme and bay leaves and cook for 5 minutes more. Pour through a sieve to remove the excess fat. Boil the red wine marinade until it is reduced by three-quarters, then add the stock. Simmer gently, skimming continuously, until the mixture thickens. Pass through a fine chinoise sieve lined with a double layer of muslin, then add the chocolate and crème de mûre.

To serve This looks best on rectangular plates. Paint a strip of the blackberry purée along the length of the plate using a pastry brush. Place a chef's square in the centre and fill it with a portion of red cabbage. Remove the square. Place some beetroot, salsify and blackberries on either side of the cabbage. Add two dragged quenelles of the blackberry purée. Then place 3 pieces of venison on top of the cabbage. Stand 2 pieces of tuile either side of the venison, leaning against the beetroot and salsify. Drizzle the sauce on top of the venison to finish.

Roast Stuffed Pheasant Breasts

with three-root mash, buttered spinach and hedgerow sauce

Pheasant breast can go dry, but not when you cook it this way. We smeared the breasts in butter and wrapped them in caul – otherwise known as pig clingfilm. Caul is great for keeping meat juicy and any butcher will supply it.

Serves 8

Hedgerow sauce
2 pheasant carcasses
50g butter
1 onion, chopped
1 celery stick, chopped
1 carrot, peeled and chopped
1 tbsp tomato purée
150ml red wine
400ml chicken stock
3 tbsp hedgerow jelly
2 bay leaves
3 sprigs of thyme
2 sprigs of flat-leaf parsley
1 sprig of rosemary

Stuffed pheasant breasts
75g butter
½ onion, finely diced
150g pork sausage meat
75g cooked chestnuts, chopped
zest of 1 lemon
4 sage leaves, finely chopped
4 pheasant breasts
1 caul

Mash and spinach
500g potatoes
500g celeriac
500g Jerusalem artichokes
110g butter
75ml double cream
250g spinach

To prepare the hedgerow sauce
Preheat the oven to 180°C/Gas 4. Remove the breasts from the pheasant, and set them aside. Chop the rest of the carcass into pieces, put it in a roasting tin and roast for 15–20 minutes.

Heat a sauté pan, add a little of the butter, then the onion, celery and carrot and fry for 3–4 minutes. Add the tomato purée and cook for 1 minute, then add the roasted pheasant carcass to the pan. Deglaze the roasting pan with the red wine, scraping up any juicy bits and pour it all into the sauté pan. Add the chicken stock, bring to the boil, then reduce the heat and simmer for 15–20 minutes. Strain into a clean saucepan and check the seasoning. Add the hedgerow jelly and fresh herbs, check the seasoning once more, then set aside until ready to serve.

the pheasant season:
In the UK, pheasants are bred to be hunted and shot – the open season for pheasant shooting runs from 1 October–1 February.

To prepare the stuffed pheasant breasts

Heat a frying pan and add a little butter and the diced onion. Cook for 2–3 minutes until the onion is just softened but not coloured. Put the sausage meat, chestnuts, lemon and sage into a bowl and mix them together well. Add the cooked onion, season with salt and black pepper and mix again. Spoon into a piping bag.

Preheat the oven to 180°C/Gas 4. Make an incision in the top end of a pheasant breast, and using a thin knife, or the end of a wooden spoon, enlarge the incision to make a pocket inside. Place the end of the piping bag into the pheasant pocket and squeeze in as much stuffing as possible. Repeat with the remaining pheasant breasts and stuffing.

Put a couple of slices of butter on the skin side of each breast, then wrap them in the caul – this will help baste the breasts when they are cooking. Roast the stuffed breasts for 12–15 minutes until they are cooked through, then leave them to rest for a few minutes.

To prepare the mash and spinach

Peel the potatoes, celeriac and Jerusalem artichokes and cut them into chunks. Put them into 3 separate pans of salted water. Bring to the boil, then reduce the heat and simmer for 10–15 minutes until all the vegetables are tender.

Drain the vegetables, return them to the pans, then place on the heat to dry them out for a couple of minutes. Pass all the vegetables through a ricer into a clean pan. Season with salt and black pepper, then add three-quarters of the butter and the cream and beat well to make a creamy, smooth mash.

Heat a frying pan and add the remaining butter and the spinach. Cook for 1 minute until the leaves are just wilted, then season with salt, black pepper and nutmeg.

To serve

Heat the sauce and whisk in the remaining butter. Place a spoonful of mash in the centre of each plate. Carve each pheasant breast into three on the diagonal and place the slices on top of the mash. Pile some spinach alongside the meat and spoon over the sauce.

County chef:
Richard Guest
Restaurant:
The Castle

The Castle at Taunton is one of Britain's most famous hotels, and chefs such as Gary Rhodes and Phil Vickery have cooked in its kitchens. Head chef Richard Guest has been at the Castle for nine years and serves the best modern British food. Most of the produce he uses in his menu comes from the surrounding countryside and the restaurant has a great reputation for food inspired by the region. Seafood comes from Brixham fish market, game from the nearby Quantock Hills and even the restaurant's bread is made from flour that is stone ground at a working mill near Wells.

Somerset

"Somerset – what a place! Cider is important here, of course, so we thought it our duty to go to the West Croft Cider Wassail, an ancient ritual that's maintained to this day in these parts. It was held on a chilly night in January, but we didn't stay chilly for long as we joined several hundred people to down pints of wonderful cider and feast on hog roast and apple cake. Everyone gathered round to bang drums, play guitars and sing traditional Wassail songs round the Wassail tree – the oldest tree in the orchard – and a very good time was had by all. Especially us – we had to leave the bikes that night. Once we'd recovered, we visited Tony and Jill Corpe's water buffalo farm – the only one in Somerset – where they produce top-quality meat as well as a range of pies and pasties. Then we met John Rowswell, a passionate market gardener who grows up to 60 varieties of vegetable including five types of beetroot, a traditional Somerset veg. Despite all this excitement, we did notice that Somerset is a very picturesque county with beautiful fertile land. There's a lovely peaceful pace to life – when they're not wassailing. "

Somerset Chicken

You get good chickens in Somerset. This is a traditional recipe that uses two local ingredients – Cheddar cheese and cider – so we didn't mess with it. Makes a really nice supper dish, served with some baked potatoes to mop up the juices.

Serves 6

6 boneless chicken breasts, skin on
3 tbsp olive oil
75g butter
2 onions, sliced
4 tbsp plain flour
2 tbsp grain mustard
2 dessert apples, peeled
  and sliced into batons

110g button mushrooms, sliced
250ml chicken stock
300ml cider
250ml double cream
1 tbsp finely chopped sage leaves
300g Cheddar cheese, grated
6 baked potatoes

Preheat the oven to 200°C/Gas 6. Season the chicken breasts with salt and black pepper. Heat a large sauté pan and add 2 tablespoons of the oil and 50g of the butter.

tip:
Cheddar is now produced all over the world, but the cheese did originally come from the village of Cheddar in Somerset and has been made since the 12th century. Legend has it that the first Cheddar was made when a milkmaid left a pail of milk in the Cheddar Gorge caves. She came back to find it had been transformed – into cheese.

Fry the chicken breasts in batches for 1–2 minutes on each side until golden. Put them into a deep-sided oven tray and roast for 25 minutes until the chicken is cooked through.

Add the remaining butter and oil to the sauté pan and cook the onions for 4–5 minutes until softened but not coloured. Add the flour and mustard to the pan and cook for a nother 2 minutes. Add the apples and button mushrooms and cook for 1 minute. Pour in the chicken stock and bring to the boil, then pour in the cider. Bring back to the boil and cook for 5 minutes. Add the cream and sage, cook for another 5 minutes, then season with salt and black pepper.

Take the chicken out of the oven and pour the sauce into the dish to cover the chicken completely. Preheat the grill to high. Sprinkle the cheese over the chicken and place under the grill for 5 minutes until the cheese is melted, golden and bubbling. Serve with jacket potatoes topped with a knob of butter.

Richard Guest's Celebration of Beef

You need top-quality beef, like they have in Somerset, for this recipe. Talk to your butcher and ask him to get you the caul (the stomach lining of a sheep, cow or pig) and the rendered beef dripping. You will also need some dariole moulds.

Serves 4

Suet dough
300g self-raising flour
150g beef suet
chopped parsley to taste
1 egg
cold water (80ml or more)

Braised oxtail
1 large oxtail, about 600g before trimming
20g rendered beef dripping
100g sliced onions or shallots
2 garlic cloves, crushed
about 500ml beef stock
1 fresh or 2 dried bay leaves
1 tsp salt and pepper

Ox heart faggots
½ ox heart
100g diced demi-sel pork
   or dry-cured streaky bacon
100g chopped shallots
chopped parsley
150g suet
1 tsp salt and pepper
soaked caul fat
beef stock for poaching the faggots

Onion and tongue gravy
30ml rendered beef dripping
200g beef (fingers of rib beef, trimmings
   from around the ribs), roughly diced
2 shallots, chopped
200ml water
75g butter, diced
1 extra shallot, finely diced
30g tongue, diced

Fillet steaks
4 x 200g top-quality beef fillets
50ml vegetable oil
50g butter

Ceps
100g dried ceps, soaked for 10 minutes
50ml cream
25g butter

Spinach
150g fresh spinach
50g butter

Carrots
24 baby carrots
100g butter
a small bunch of flat-leaf parsley

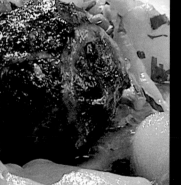

To prepare the suet dough
Put the flour and suet in the mixing bowl. Mix in the seasoning and parsley. Stir in the egg and then the cold water, a little at a time. The amount of water will vary from batch to batch of flour. Mix, working it as little as possible until a fairly soft elastic dough is obtained. For storage purposes, divide the dough into 3, roll out into sausages, wrap and refrigerate.

To make the braised oxtail

Trim off most of the surface fat and cut through the natural joints in the tail – about every 4–5cm. Heat the dripping in a frying pan large enough to contain the oxtail in a single layer. When it's nearly smoking, add the meat. Brown thoroughly on all sides. Don't hurry or skimp this stage, because it's critical to the final taste. When it's almost ready, put in the onions and let them soften, then the garlic. Take the pan off the heat and then transfer the meat, onions and garlic to a clean pot. Discard the dripping in the frying pan. Deglaze with a cup of water, scrape any sediment from the bottom of the pan and add it to the meat. Cover the meat with stock. Boil, skim the excess fat from the surface and turn down to simmer. Add the bay leaf and seasoning, then cook until the meat comes away from the bone, topping up with stock if necessary. This should take about 3½ hours. Once the meat is cooked, reduce stock to about 200ml.

To make the puddings

Butter and flour the inside of the dariole moulds and put a circle of non-stick baking parchment in the bottom. Roll out the dough to about 3mm thick and line each mould so that the dough overhangs the edges. Roll out the rest of the pastry for the lids. Fill the moulds with warm oxtail. Add the lids and crimp the edges to seal. Cover with buttered foil. Place the puddings in a pan and add boiling water to reach about half way up the sides of the moulds. Cover the pan, steam the puddings for 10–15 minutes and turn them out.

To prepare the ox heart faggots

Split the heart open and trim any pieces of fat. Cut out the arteries and veins, which are gristly and chop the meat coarsely. If you have a mincer, set it to medium and mince the ox heart with the pork or bacon, shallots, parsley, suet, salt and pepper. Otherwise, blitz the mixture in a food processor. Mix well by hand. For each faggot, lay a piece of caul about 20cm square on the work surface. Form a ball of mixture about the size of a golf ball and wrap it in caul. Make sure you only wrap it around the faggot once, otherwise it can become too chewy. Chill and then poach the faggots for 10 minutes in beef stock when needed.

To make the onion and tongue gravy

Heat the dripping until very hot. Add the meat in a single layer and fry until well coloured. If the meat is of good quality it won't sweat or stew. Add the shallots and continue cooking until they start to brown. Strain off all the fat. Deglaze with a little water and scrape any sediment from the bottom of the pan. Add the rest of the water, boil, skim, season and set to one side of the cooker. Leave for no more than 20 minutes to extract the flavour from the meat. Strain through a sieve into a clean pan without pressing or forcing the meat or shallots. The aim is to obtain a clean-flavoured jus. To finish the gravy, whisk in cubed butter to emulsify it and add the raw shallots and the tongue.

To cook the fillet steaks

Preheat the oven to 180°C/Gas 4. Pat the steaks with kitchen paper to remove any moisture. Heat an ovenproof pan until searingly hot and add the oil. When this is about to smoke, add the butter, followed by the steaks. Seal the steaks for about 1 minute on each side and season. Remove the pan form the heat and transfer to the oven. For rare meat, cook the steaks for 4–6 minutes, depending on their thickness Leave to rest for 5 minutes before serving

To cook the vegetables

Drain the ceps and put them in a frying pan with the butter. Once coloured, add the cream, season to taste and reduce a little until ready to serve. Wash the spinach thoroughly. Heat the butter in a pan until melted and throw in the spinach. Cover with a lid and wilt for 2–3 minutes, no longer. Blanche the carrots in boiling water for 1 minute, drain and set aside. Melt the butter in a pan and add the baby carrots. Leave to poach and soften to al dente for 3 minutes. Be careful not to burn the butter. When ready to serve, add the chopped parsley and season lightly to taste.

to serve:
To assemble, put one faggot on a bed of spinach on each plate. Turn out the pudding from its mould, lay several of the carrots on it with a few more to one side. Slice the fillet on a slant and arrange on the plate. Spoon some ceps to one side of it. Pour a cordon of gravy around tthe meat and the pudding.

Water Buffalo Rossini
with bone-marrow crust and red and golden beetroot

This is a classy dish based on the famous tournedos Rossini – a great last from the past dragged into the 21st century with wonderful Somerset ingredients. Believe us when we tell you that it's worth the faff because it tastes great. Buffalo is low in fat and cholesterol so a very healthy meat.

Serves 4

Water buffalo Rossini

800g water buffalo fillet, room temperature
50g cooked bone marrow
50g dried white breadcrumbs
2 tbsp finely chopped curly parsley
100g butter, softened
3 tbsp olive oil
1 garlic bulb
4 slices white bread
2 duck livers, trimmed
and soaked in 50ml Madeira
12 small wild mushrooms, cleaned
1 tbsp truffle oil
75ml Somerset cider brandy
2 tbsp port
200ml beef or veal stock

Fondant potatoes

4 good potatoes
150g butter
75–110ml chicken stock

Beetroot

2 Detroit beetroot,
washed but unpeeled
2 Candy beetroot,
washed but unpeeled
2 Bolivar beetroot,
washed but unpeeled
2 Golden beetroot,
washed but unpeeled
2 lemons, juiced
1–2 tbsp caster sugar

To cook the beetroot

tip:

It's important to cook beetroot with the skin on or the colour – and flavour – leaks out. The juices really stain your hands so wear rubber gloves when peeling beets. If you can't find these beetroots, buy whatever is available. Some supermarkets stock yellow beets.

Put the red and golden beetroot in separate pans of salted water – it's important to cook them separately so the red doesn't taint the golden beetroot. Bring to the boil, cover and simmer for 45–60 minutes until tender. Leave to cool slightly, then very carefully cut them into squares, keeping them the same size. You need to get 4 squares from each beetroot. Keeping the colours separate, place the squares back in the cooking pans ready to warm through just before serving. Whisk the lemon juice and sugar together to make the dressing for the beetroot and season with salt and black pepper. Divide into two separate bowls. When ready to serve, warm the beetroot and toss each colour in its bowl of dressing.

To cook the fondant potatoes

Peel the potatoes and cut off the tops and bottoms so they are flat at both ends. Cut out rounds of potato with a pastry cutter and trim off the sharp corners to make nice barrel shapes. Melt the butter in a pan, then add the potatoes and cook for 3–4 minutes over a gentle heat until golden.

Turn the potatoes, putting them back on the same place in the pan and cook for another 3–4 minutes until the other side is golden. Carefully ladle in some stock – we warn you, it will spit – then pour in more until the potatoes are nearly covered. Cover and simmer gently for 20–25 minutes or until cooked. Keep warm until ready to serve.

To prepare the water buffalo

First the steaks need to be formed into lovely round shapes. Place the meat on a sheet of clingfilm and roll it up as tightly as possible to form a neat sausage shape. Twist the ends up like a big toffee. Put the meat in the fridge to rest for at least 2 hours.

Mix the bone marrow, breadcrumbs, parsley and 50g of the softened butter together in a bowl. Spread the mixture out thinly on a sheet of greaseproof paper on a baking tray – think biscuit – and place in the fridge until set. Preheat the oven to 200°C/Gas 6. Slice the top from the garlic bulb and dot with butter, salt and black pepper. Wrap it in foil and place in the oven for 30 minutes until soft. Set aside, still wrapped in the foil.

Take the buffalo fillet out of the fridge and slice into 4 steaks, about 2cm thick. Season them with salt and black pepper. Heat a frying pan, add a little of the buffalo fat (or butter and oil), then put in the steaks and seal on each side for 20–30 seconds until browned. Transfer the steaks to a baking tray and keep the frying pan with the meat juices.

Take the marrow mixture out of the fridge and cut it into discs slightly smaller than the steaks. Place one on top of each steak and place them in the oven for 6–8 minutes. This will give medium-rare meat, but adjust the timing to your taste. Cut out 4 rounds of white bread with a pastry cutter, making them just slightly larger than the steaks. Heat some olive oil and butter in a frying pan and fry the bread until golden. Remove the meat from the oven. Put the fried croutons on warm plates and top each one with a steak. As the steak rests, the crouton will absorb all the resting juices.

Meanwhile, take the livers out of the Madeira, keeping the liquid. Using the pan with the meat juices, cook the duck livers for 45–60 seconds on each side. Remove, leaving the juices in the pan. Rest the duck livers for a minute before slicing them in half and placing a piece on each steak stack. Add the mushrooms to the pan and sauté for 1–2 minutes until just tender, then add the truffle oil and season with salt and black pepper. Set those on top of the duck liver. Add the Madeira to the pan and flame to deglaze, then add the brandy and port and reduce by half. Add the stock, bring to a simmer and cook until reduced and thickened slightly. Whisk in the remaining butter, then season with salt and black pepper.

To serve

Set some fondant potatoes alongside the buffalo stack. Place 4 squares of beetroot across the top of the plate – running lightest in colour to darkest. Pop the juicy roasted garlic out of the cloves on to the meat and spoon the sauce over the top of the buffalo stack and around the plate.

County chef:
Matt Davies
Restaurant:
The Moat House

The Moat House, in the village of Acton Trussell, isa long-established, extremely successful restaurant. It has four AA stars, has been Michelin listed for the last ten years and a Taste of Staffordshire winner five years in a row.

Executive chef Matt always knew he wanted to be a chef and grew up cooking for his mum and siblings. At the Moat House, he uses a range of locally sourced produce to create his versions of traditional dishes and modern British food.

"This is pick-your-own land. There are so many great farms where you can go along, pick what you want and take it home, banging fresh, to your kitchen. We went to Essington Fruit Farm and did exactly that – picked some tasty gooseberries to make a sauce for our roast chicken. Did you know that Dr Johnson was born in Lichfield and lived there until he was 28? He encouraged Boswell to visit the county so he could experience 'proper genteel English life'. How about that?

We liked it here, too. We got a great welcome and people were really helpful. They kept telling us about the London Road Bakehouse in Stoke and how good their bread is. They are one of the last bakeries to use a coal-fired oven – it's been there for 130 years – so we had to take a look. Sure enough the bread is fantastic, as are the ladies running it. Staffordshire oatcakes were another must, we were told, and we had to go to the Hole-in-the-Wall shop in Hanley. It's just like it sounds – they sell oatcakes from a front room shop. People come from miles around and the oatcakes really are good. "

Staffordshire

Oatcakes
with bacon, mushrooms and cheese

We cooked this dish in Lichfield and to our great surprise one of our heroes appeared out of nowhere – the singer Tony Christie. Remember him? One of his hits was 'Is this the way to Amarillo?'. Anyway, he sampled an oatcake, loved it, and made our day.

Serves 12

225g fine oatmeal

100g wholemeal flour

100g plain flour

1 tsp quick-action yeast

pinch of salt

825ml water

1 tbsp baking powder

1 tbsp vegetable oil

24 rashers of streaky bacon

300g mature Cheddar cheese

1 tbsp olive oil

150g chestnut mushrooms, halved

Place the oatmeal, wholemeal flour, plain flour, yeast and salt in a bowl and mix together. Add the water and mix to a batter. Cover and set aside for at least 3–4 hours – the longer the better, but no more than 8 hours. Mix once more, then whisk in the baking powder.

Heat a medium-size frying pan, add a little of the vegetable oil and a ladleful of batter. Swirl quickly to coat the pan, then return to the heat. Cook over a medium heat until you see bubbles appear on the surface of the oatcake. Flip and cook for another minute on the other side. Remove the oatcake and place on some baking parchment, then repeat until the batter is used up. You can stack the oatcakes with a piece of parchment between each one.

info:

Staffordshire oatcakes aren't the usual kind, but more like a leavened oaty pancake. They can be served hot with a savoury filling as here or as a pud with strawberries and cream and other delights.

Meanwhile, heat the grill to high. Place the bacon on a grill tray and grill on both sides until browned and crispy. Heat a frying pan, add the olive oil and mushrooms and cook for 3–4 minutes until golden and cooked through. Return a cooked oatcake to a dry, medium-hot frying pan and sprinkle grated cheese over half of it. Cook for a few minutes until the cheese starts to melt, then top with a couple of slices of bacon and a few mushrooms and flip the other half over the top. Cook for 1 minute, then serve.

Repeat until all the oatcakes, bacon, mushrooms and cheese are finished!

Matt Davies's Fillet of Tamworth Pork

with mousseline potatoes, creamed courgettes and organic lager sauce

Matt Davies is a great classic cook and his mastery of culinary techniques really showed in this dish. He believes that many of the traditional rules are still worth following and if this dish is anything to go by, he's right.

Serves 4

Pork
4 x 175g fillets of pork, trimmed
8 slices of prosciutto
1 handful of finely chopped chervil

Mousseline potatoes
1.5kg Wilja potatoes
100ml double cream
120g butter

Carrots and onions
12 baby carrots and 12 baby onions
butter
olive oil

Lager sauce
olive oil
150g shallots, finely chopped
1 x 300ml bottle Pilsner lager
250ml chicken stock
250ml beef stock
300ml double cream

Creamed courgettes
4 medium courgettes
butter
100ml double cream
250g mature Cheddar cheese,
  grated

To prepare the pork
Wrap each pork fillet in two slices of prosciutto ham, and then roll it up tightly in clingfilm to form a cylindrical shape. Chill in the fridge for at least an hour, or if possible overnight, to set the pork before cooking. Poach the wrapped pork fillets in a sous-vide water bath at about 95°C for around 14 minutes (see page 68 for more on this). Take out of the water and rest for 8 minutes, then remove the clingfilm and keep the pork warm.

To cook the mousseline potatoes
Peel, wash and rewash the potatoes, then cut them into equal pieces. Cook in salted water until tender, 18–20 minutes. Drain the potatoes, put them back into the pan and place on the heat to dry them out. Be careful that they don't catch and burn. Place them through a fine potato ricer. Add the cream and butter, season to taste, and whisk quickly to make soft fluffy potatoes. Cover and keep warm.

To cook the carrots and onions

Peel and wash the carrots and cook in simmering salted water until just tender. Drain, add a little butter and keep warm.

to serve:

Using a very sharp knife, carve the pork fillets into equal slices. Place a little of the creamed courgette mix on one side of a warm plate and some potato on the other. t slices of the pork fillet over the courgette mix and finish with the roast shallots and carrots. Pour over a little of the sauce and garnish with chopped chervil and crispy

Preheat the oven to 180°C/Gas 4. Peel the baby onions and put them on a small roasting tray. Add a little olive oil and sea salt and roast until just cooked. Keep warm.

To make the lager sauce

Heat a little olive oil in a pan, add the shallots and cook until they are soft but not coloured. Pour in the lager and reduce until the liquid is nearly all evaporated, then add both stocks and reduce by two-thirds. Add the cream and reduce again until the sauce coats the back of a spoon. Season to taste with salt and white pepper and keep warm.

To prepare the creamed courgettes

Wash and grate 2 of the courgettes and cook in a little butter for 3 minutes. Add the cream and reduce until thickened, then stir in the grated cheese until melted into the sauce. Cut the rest of the courgettes into barrel shapes and fry them in a little butter until just tender,

Roast Chicken and Sage and Onion Stuffing
with chips, gooseberry sauce and sausage meatballs

This is a prime example of 'if it ain't broke, don't fix it'. There's nothing better than a good roast chicken, as we're sure you'll agree. It's well worth making your own stuffing – this is Mrs Beeton's recipe.

Serves 6

tip: *If the broad beans are really young and tender you can just pod them and cook. Usually, though, it is best to remove the pale skin from each bean, revealing the bright green beauty underneath.*

Chicken and stuffing

4 medium onions, quartered
8 sage leaves
125g fresh breadcrumbs
40g butter, plus extra
for coating the chickens
1 egg yolk
pinch of nutmeg
2 really good free-range
chickens, about 2kg each

Gooseberry sauce

100ml water
4 tbsp caster sugar
zest of 1 lemon
250g gooseberries,
topped and tailed
300ml white wine
300ml chicken juices
25g unsalted butter

Chips

4 large old potatoes, like
King Edward, Maris Piper,
Desirée or Cyprus if you're
feeling flush
vegetable oil

Broad beans

500g broad beans, podded
and skins removed
1 tbsp olive oil
25g butter
4 rashers of smoked streaky bacon,
cut into lardons

Sausage meatballs

3–4 good quality
Staffordshire pork sausages
1 tbsp olive oil

To cook the chickens

Preheat the oven to 180°C/Gas 4. Place the onions in a pan of boiling water to blanch for 5 minutes. Add the sage leaves for the last minute so they wilt. Put the drained onions and sage leaves into a food processor, add the breadcrumbs, butter, seasoning, egg yolk and nutmeg. Blitz until just combined – you don't want a paste. Pack the stuffing into the neck cavity and body of the chickens.

Rub the chickens with butter and season all over with sea salt flakes and ground black pepper. Place in a roasting tin, breast-side up, and add just enough water to cover the bottom of the roasting tin. Cover with tented foil and place into the oven. Cooking times vary according to the size of the bird. Cook for 30 minutes per 500g, allowing for the weight of the stuffing. Remove the foil 20 minutes before the end of the cooking time and strain off the juices. You will need these skimmed juices when making the gooseberry sauce. Return the chicken to the oven and finish cooking them uncovered so the skin will go crispy. Leave to rest for 20 minutes before carving.

To make the gooseberry sauce

Heat the water in a pan, add the sugar and stir until it has dissolved. Add the lemon zest, mix and boil for a few minutes to thicken slightly. Add the gooseberries and poach gently for about 3 minutes. Leave to cool in the syrup. When the gooseberries are cool, pass them through a sieve to make a purée and set aside, reserving both the purée and the syrup. Pour the white wine into another saucepan and season with a little salt and pepper. Boil hard until reduced by half. Add the chicken juices and continue boiling until reduced by half. Remove from the heat and stir in the butter to give the sauce a nice sheen. Add the gooseberry purée and a little of the syrup as well if you like. Season to taste.

To make the chips

Peel the potatoes and cut them into chips, not too thick and not too thin, and wash them under cold water to get rid of the starch. If you have time, soak the chips in cold water overnight. Blot dry on kitchen roll. The secret of good chips is to cook them twice and you need a deep-fryer or a chip pan with a thermometer. Heat the oil to 130°C. Cook the chips in batches for about 10 minutes – they will not brown but should cook though to the middle. Set aside on kitchen paper and leave to cool – they can be left for several hours at this stage. Heat the oil up to 190°C and cook the chips again until crispy and golden – about 5 minutes. We love chips…. who doesn't? Go on spoil yourself.

To cook the broad beans and the sausage meatballs

Blanch the beans in boiling water until cooked. This takes about 5 minutes. Then plunge them into ice-cold water and set aside. When almost ready to serve, heat the oil and butter in a frying pan and fry the pieces of bacon until crispy. Warm the beans through in the hot bacon fat and season with a little black pepper.

The sausage meatballs make a nice garnish. Skin the sausages and form the meat into small balls the size of a walnut. Heat the oil in a frying pan and fry the balls until golden.

To serve

Carve slices from the breasts and legs of the chickens and place some on each plate. Spoon the broad beans alongside. Pile the chips into a little basket or bowl. Place a spoonful of stuffing to one side with a few sausage meatballs. Pour the gooseberry sauce over the chicken.

County chef:
Chris Lee
Restaurant:
The Bildeston Crown

Chris Lee runs The Bildeston Crown, an original 15th-century coaching inn, with his wife Hayley. They currently hold three AA Rosettes and Chris won the Up and Coming Chef of the Year award from the Good Food Guide in 2007. He is an ambitious and imaginative cook and creates some very inventive dishes, many of which use the high-quality local produce. Chris believes that Britain produces great food and is proud to create dishes from the ingredients on his doorstep.

Suffolk

"Suffolk is a really beautiful, rural county. We found the people there very hospitable and they loved talking about food – our favourite subject! One of the highlights was a visit to Jimmy Butler's Blythburgh Farm where he raises free-range pork. It's the largest independent pork producer in the country but Jimmy still manages to let his pigs live naturally. He really cares about them and we saw the lovely animals rooting in the soil and playing with their companions. And the meat tastes fantastic.

A first for us was a ferreting trip with Johnnie the Ferret Man. This is a way of catching rabbits by sending a ferret down into the warren to drive the rabbits out. It's a traditional method and the most humane. What tickled us was that the ferreter starts by putting a lady ferret down the hole. If she doesn't come out, he sends a male down after her. We also went to Pakenham water mill, the only working water mill in Suffolk. There's been a mill there for 1,000 years and they are still milling flour. We got some for making our oatcakes. "

Suffolk Pork Chops
with cider and caramelised apples

Apples are a traditional accompaniment for pork and this is a good way of cooking them as a change from apple sauce. Try these apples with roast pork, too.

Serves 4

4 pork chops

4 tsp sea salt flakes

2 onions, finely chopped

150g smoked bacon, diced

1 bouquet garni (celery, parsley, bay leaves and thyme)

300g button mushrooms

300g shallots, blanched for 10 minutes, then drained and refreshed

500ml Suffolk cider

4 Cox's apples, peeled, cored and quartered

4 tbsp muscovado sugar

4 tsp Suffolk mustard

400ml double cream

Roll the fat of the pork chops in the salt flakes – this will help to colour and crisp the fat. Preheat a griddle pan and a large non-stick frying pan. You'll be cooking in both at once, but don't worry, it's easy.

Stand the pork chops fat-side down on the hot griddle pan. You may have to hold the chops with tongs to keep them upright. Then brown the chops on both sides so they have nice striped markings.

In the large non-stick frying pan, sauté the onion and the bacon until slightly coloured. Add the bouquet garni, button mushrooms and shallots to the onion and bacon and leave to sweat for 3–4 minutes. Add the cider to the frying pan, bring it to the boil, then add the pork chops and any juices from the griddle pan and cook for 10–15 minutes until the chops are cooked through. Keep the griddle pan on the stove for the apples.

Dust the apples with sugar, place them on the griddle and cook for 5–10 minutes until they are caramelised and coloured but not falling to bits. Remove the pork chops from the pan and set aside to rest.

tip:
Griddling the chops first to seal in the flavour and then poaching them in the sauce really does make the meat tender and juicy. Please, please keep to the timings and you won't go wrong.

Bring the remaining ingredients in the frying pan up to a rapid boil, add the mustard and cream and cook until reduced. This should take another 4–5 minutes.

To serve
Serve the pork chops with the sauce and caramelised apples. Some carrots and mash make good accompaniments

Chris Lee's Roasted Breast of Mallard
with Clementine espuma, gizzard sausage and dauphinoise potatoes

Ask your butcher to keep the hearts and gizzards for you. You may also want him to remove the breasts and bone the legs; just make sure you collect the bones.

Serves 4

2 wild mallards (or other small ducks)
200g kale, leaves picked off and washed
butter

Heart stew
400g duck hearts
500ml red wine
3 sprigs of thyme
2 garlic cloves
butter
110g each diced celeriac,
    carrot and onion
1 litre demi-glace
1 handful of chopped parsley

Clementine espuma
10 clementines
1 clove
1 star anise
1 cardamom pod
25ml brandy
orange juice

Duck consommé
2 duck carcasses
150g mirepoix (carrot, onion,
    celery and leeks, all roughly chopped)
butter
1 tbsp tomato purée
150ml red wine

2 egg whites
1 duck breast

Dauphinoise potatoes
4 large Maris Piper potatoes
110ml milk
110ml double cream
pinch of nutmeg
1 garlic clove

Squash purée
1 chestnut or butternut squash
110g butter
50ml hot chicken stock

Duck legs
4 duck legs
1 litre duck fat
2 sprigs of thyme
2 garlic cloves
flour
1 beaten egg
breadcrumbs

Gizzard sausage
125g gizzards
1 chicken breast
1 egg white
200ml double cream
4 slices Parma ham

tip:

You can make the dauphinoise ahead of time and follow this tip for serving. When the potatoes are cooked, place another dish the same size on top with a heavy weight to press the potatoes down. Leave for a couple of hours. Once set, turn the dauphinoise out on to a chopping board and cut into 5 x 2.5cm wedges. Warm through in the oven for 5–8 minutes before serving.

To prepare the heart stew

Trim the white bits off the top of the hearts and cut them into 4. Marinate the hearts in the red wine, thyme and garlic for 24 hours, then remove and dry them. Quickly sauté the hearts in butter, then add the vegetables. Pour in the demi-glace and cook until tender. Finish with chopped parsley.

To make the clementine espuma

Put all the ingredients into a pan and simmer until the clementines are completely soft. Pour everything into a blender and blitz until smooth, then pass through a fine sieve. Pour liquid into an espuma gun and charge with CO_2 cylinders. Keep warm.

To prepare the duck consommé

Preheat the oven to 140°C/Gas 1. Roast the bones for 3 hours and put them to one side. Sweat the mirepoix vegetables in butter until golden brown, add the tomato purée and cook for 2–3 minutes. Then add the duck bones and red wine and cover with water. Gently simmer for 4–5 hours, skimming any fat off the top. Pass the mixture through a sieve to remove the bones and mirepoix. Return the liquid to the pan and reduce it slowly until it turns a deep dark colour. In a food processor blitz the egg whites and duck breast and whisk this into the liquid. Slowly bring to a simmer, making sure you don't boil or stir. After around 10 minutes the egg white mixture should have floated to the top, bringing any impurities with it. Carefully skim this off the top without disturbing the consommé below. Gently pass the remaining liquid through muslin to leave a clear consommé.

To make the dauphinoise potatoes and squash purée

Preheat the oven to 180°C/Gas 4. Peel and finely slice the potatoes. Heat the milk, cream, nutmeg and garlic in a pan to infuse the flavours, taking care not to boil. Grease a 12.5cm x 7.5cm x 5cm dish and layer in the potato slices. Remove the garlic from the milk mixture and pour the milk over the potatoes. Cover with foil and cook in the oven for 45 minutes to 1 hour. Peel and deseed the squash, slice it finely and sweat in the butter until soft. Place in a blender and blitz, adding a little of the chicken stock at a time until you have a smooth purée, then pass through a fine sieve. Reheat before serving.

To prepare the duck legs

Preheat the oven to 140°C/Gas 1. Split the duck legs into thighs and drumsticks, place them in an oven dish and cover with the duck fat. Add the thyme and garlic and cover with greaseproof paper. Bake for 2–3 hours until the meat is falling off the bone. Carefully remove, keeping the pieces intact. Keep the fat, as it can be used again for the gizzards. Put the drumsticks in the fridge to set. Once they are firm, trim into the desired shape. Pick the meat from the thighs, discarding the bones, fat and skin. Finely shred the meat and chill it in the fridge. Roll the thigh meat into four balls roughly the size of a ping-pong ball and put back into the fridge to chill. When ready to serve, dip in flour, then beaten egg and breadcrumbs, and then into the egg and breadcrumbs again. Heat a deep-fat fryer to 180°C. Add the thigh balls and fry for 2–3 minutes until golden and heated through.

to serve:

Place a wedge of dauphinoise on each plate. Slice the mallard breasts and lay some on top of the potato. Put a confit thigh ball next to it. Add a small pile of kale with a slice of the gizzard mousse on top, followed by the duck drumstick. Smear a spoonful of the purée on the opposite side of the plate. Pour the hot consommé into a shot glass and spoon the clementine espuma on top. Serve with a small portion of the heart stew alongside.

To make the gizzard sausage

Sprinkle sea salt on to the gizzards and leave for 5 hours, then rinse. Confit the gizzards until tender, using the same method as for the duck legs. Remove from the fat and cool. In a food processor blitz the chicken breast into a paste, then add the egg white. Slowly add the cream. Mix this mousse with the cold gizzards. Place the mixture on clingfilm and roll into a long sausage about 20cm long. Steam or poach for about 20 minutes, then leave to cool before removing the clingfilm. The sausage should be set. Finally wrap the Parma ham around the sausage and cut into four even pieces.

To prepare the mallard breast and kale

Pan-fry the mallard breast and gizzard sausage, finishing them in the oven for about 2 minutes. Blanch the kale for about 2 minutes in boiling water, refresh in iced water and drain. When ready to serve, sauté with butter and season.

Stuffed Saddle of Rabbit
with cranberry and cheese oatcakes

Don't be scared of cooking rabbit. It's delicious when cooked properly and you'll be surprised how much meat there is. You'll need two rabbits for this recipe – ask your butcher to joint them and bone the saddles. This is great served with some braised red cabbage

Serves 4

tip: To get the best from rabbit, have it jointed so you can cook the parts in different ways. The saddle is the tenderest meat, so requires much less cooking than the legs or shoulders, which are better braised.

Rabbit

rabbit carcasses, cut into chunks, bone in
2 tbsp olive oil
250ml dry white wine
1 shallot, finely diced
1 carrot, finely diced
1 celery stick, finely diced
250ml chicken stock
1 bay leaf
sea salt flakes and ground white pepper
butter
4 boned rabbit saddles,
rubbed with olive oil and seasoned
250g pancetta or thin streaky bacon
250g baby spinach

Mushroom duxelles

125g unsalted butter
3 shallots, finely chopped
500g mushrooms, finely chopped
15g dried porcini mushrooms, soaked
in a little boiling water
1 tbsp double cream
2 tbsp finely chopped parsley
1 egg white

Oatcakes

2 tbsp lard
100g medium oatmeal
100g wholemeal flour
1 tsp bicarbonate of soda
½ teaspoon salt
1 tbsp dried cranberries
1 tbsp strong cheese, finely grated
8 tbsp boiling water

Game chips

a couple of good potatoes, peeled
sunflower oil for frying

To make the rabbit gravy

Sauté the rabbit chunks in olive oil until browned. Place the browned rabbit in a saucepan and add the wine, shallot, carrot, celery, stock, bay leaf and seasoning. Cover and simmer until the meat is falling off the bones. Strain and set aside the bones and meat. Reduce the stock from the poached rabbit until it has thickened and the taste intensified, then whisk in a little butter and you will have a nice little gravy.

Once the bones are cool enough to handle, pick off any meat, chop finely and set aside for the duxelles.

To make the duxelles

Melt the butter in a frying pan, add the shallots and sweat until translucent. Add the fresh mushrooms and sweat with the lid on for another 5 minutes. Add the dried porcini, soaking juices and the cream. Stir and cook with the lid off until the juices have almost gone. Allow to cool and then stir in the parsley, egg white and about 300g of the poached rabbit meat. Place in a food processor and blitz, not too fine as you want some texture. Taste and add the seasoning. Set aside.

To prepare the saddle of rabbit

Preheat the oven to 180°C/Gas 4. Lay the strips of pancetta side by side until you have a blanket the same width as the rabbit saddle. You will need 4 of these. Place a layer of spinach leaves on each one. Close to one end, lay a rabbit saddle. On top of this place a sausage shape of the duxelles – it should be about the same size as the rabbit. Roll this up tightly and place on to an oiled baking sheet with the join facing downwards. Repeat to make the other 3 parcels. Roast in the preheated oven for about 15 minutes. If the pancetta hasn't coloured enough, finish under the grill.

To make the oatcakes

Preheat the oven to 200°C/Gas 6. Melt the lard in a small pan. In a bowl place the oatmeal, flour, bicarb, salt, cranberries and cheese. Pour on the melted lard and work the mixture into crumbs. Add the boiling water and mix until a dough forms. Roll this out to a thickness of about 0.5cm, then cut into oatcakes using a circular pastry cutter.

Line a baking tray with silicone baking parchment, place the oatcakes on the tray and bake for 10 minutes until they are starting to brown at the edges. Cool on a wire rack.

To cook the game chips

Slice the potatoes very finely on a mandolin. Fry in hot oil until golden, then season and serve.

To serve

Slice the rabbit saddle carefully and serve on warm plates. Stack the oatcakes and game chips in neat piles and dress with a little of the gravy.

County chef:
Ross Pavey
Restaurant:
Moonrakers

Moonrakers is in Alfriston, often said to be Sussex's most beautiful village. It's nothing to do with James Bond – the restaurant is named after a local legend about smugglers. Head chef Ross Pavey believes in honest, top-quality food that isn't too fussed over – he likes a carrot to look like a carrot. He is a great supporter of local farmers and has set up a website profiling various Sussex producers to help other cooks and chefs to find the best the county has to offer. He tries to get as many of the ingredients used in the restaurant as possible from a 25-mile radius and uses free-range produce whenever he can.

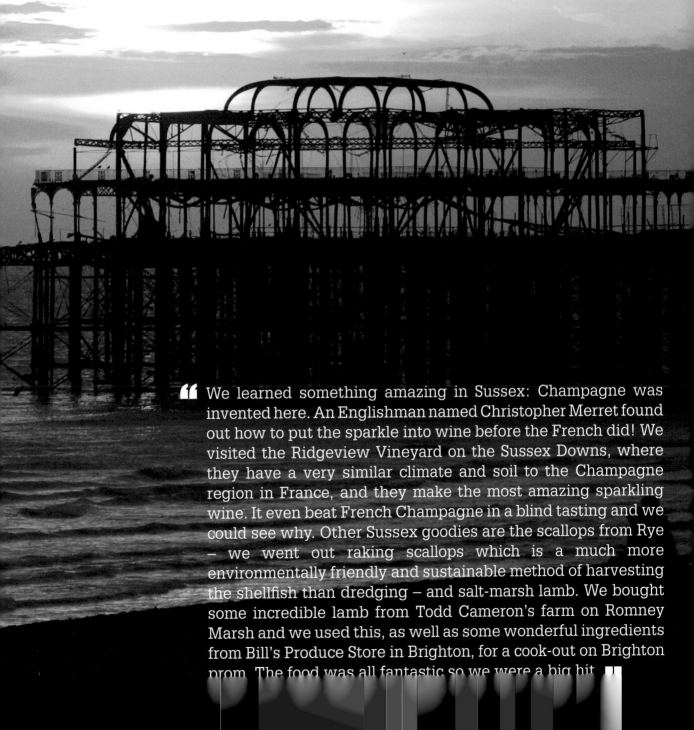

East Sussex

"We learned something amazing in Sussex: Champagne was invented here. An Englishman named Christopher Merret found out how to put the sparkle into wine before the French did! We visited the Ridgeview Vineyard on the Sussex Downs, where they have a very similar climate and soil to the Champagne region in France, and they make the most amazing sparkling wine. It even beat French Champagne in a blind tasting and we could see why. Other Sussex goodies are the scallops from Rye — we went out raking scallops which is a much more environmentally friendly and sustainable method of harvesting the shellfish than dredging — and salt-marsh lamb. We bought some incredible lamb from Todd Cameron's farm on Romney Marsh and we used this, as well as some wonderful ingredients from Bill's Produce Store in Brighton, for a cook-out on Brighton prom. The food was all fantastic so we were a big hit.

Lamb and Barley Hotpot

Be patient with this one and let it cook for a long time. The meat will shrink back off the bones of the shanks and taste great. If you have an Aga you could leave it in the oven to cook overnight.

Serves 6

6 lamb shanks
2 tbsp olive oil
2 onions, roughly chopped
3 carrots, peeled and roughly chopped
½ swede or turnip, peeled and
   cut into small chunks
4 garlic cloves, roughly chopped
2 tbsp finely chopped rosemary

2 bay leaves
2 sprigs of thyme, finely chopped
2 tbsp tomato purée
250g pearl barley
1½ litres chicken stock
2–3 tbsp mint jelly
3 tbsp roughly chopped flat-leaf parsley

Preheat the oven to 150°C/Gas 2. Season the lamb shanks with salt and black pepper. Heat a large ovenproof casserole, dish, add the oil and lamb shanks and cook them on each side until golden brown. Remove the lamb and add the onions, carrot, swede or turnip and garlic and cook for 2–3 minutes. Add the herbs and tomato purée and cook for another minute.

Add the pearl barley and stock to the pan, then the lamb shanks and bring everything to a simmer. Cover tightly, transfer to the oven and cook for as long as possible – 3–6 hours is fine. Take the casserole out of the oven and add the mint jelly and parsley. Check the seasoning before serving.

tip:
Barley usually needs to be soaked overnight before using – check the packet – but in this recipe it is cooked for so long it's fine without soaking. Barley is a great flavour carrier – try putting a bit of spice in the soaking water.

Ross Pavey's Wild Turbot
with chicken wings, beetroot and celeriac fondant

Ross loves to put strange bedfellows together in his dishes and has the knack of making his combinations succeed. We've enjoyed his food on a number of occasions. Turbot is the king of fish and for this recipe Ross used a wild turbot of the very highest quality.

Serves 4

8 beetroots

vegetable oil

2 medium celeriac

1.2 litres chicken stock

thyme sprigs

110g butter

rapeseed oil

8 free-range chicken wings

knob of butter

1 carrot, peeled and diced

thyme

1kg turbot fillets

110ml double cream

2 tsp lecithin powder

1 bunch of sorrel cress

To cook the beetroot purée and crisps

Preheat the oven to 180°C/Gas 4. Take 6 of the beetroot and scrub them, leaving the skin on. Wrap them in foil, place on a baking tray and bake for 2 hours. Once cooked, remove the foil and leave to cool before peeling. Chop the beetroot into small pieces and blitz to a fine purée in a food processor. Set aside and keep warm until ready to serve.

To make the crisps, peel the other 2 beetroot. Using a mandolin, slice them on the thinnest setting you can. Heat a frying pan and fill with vegetable oil. Drop in the beetroot slices. They should only take around 2 minutes to cook, but a good check is when only the smallest bubbles are left on the beetroot. This is an indication that all the moisture has evaporated. Remove the crisps and blot the excess oil on kitchen paper.

To make the celeriac fondant

Chop one celeriac into small pieces and put it into a pan with half the chicken stock, a sprig of thyme, some butter and a little water to cover if needed. Reduce until soft and the liquid has evaporated. Take out the thyme and blitz the celeriac in a food blender until smooth.

Using a pastry cutter, cut the remaining celeriac into rounds measuring 2 x 5cm to make the fondant slices – one per portion. Place the pieces of celeriac in a pan with a little chicken stock, thyme and butter and simmer gently until soft.

tip:
Lecithin, used here for the foam, is an emulsifier and helps the foam hold together. It's available from health food stores and on-line culinary suppliers.

To cook the chicken wings
Heat 1 tablespoon of rapeseed oil in a pan with a knob of butter and cook the chicken
wings until caramelised. Add the diced carrot and a few sprigs of thyme, cook for a few
minutes more, then cover with the rest of the chicken stock. Reduce the heat and simmer
until cooked through. Remove the chicken, but keep the stock, and cut the bones out from
the wings.

To cook the turbot
Heat a pan with some rapeseed oil. Season the turbot fillet with salt and pepper and place
in the pan, skin-side down. Turn the heat down and leave the fish until it is nearly cooked
through. Turn it over and take off the heat. The residual heat in the pan will finish cooking
the turbot.

To prepare the foam sauce
Return the stock from the chicken to the heat. Once it is hot, add the cream and 2 teaspoons
of lecithin powder. This acts as an emulsifier and helps to hold the foam. Take a hand blender
and continue agitating the sauce until a foam is formed.

To serve
Using a piping bag, draw a straight line of the beetroot purée across the plate, just off centre.
Place two separate spoonfuls of the celeriac purée at one end of the plate and sit a chicken
wing on each. Top each with a beetroot crisp. Place one piece of turbot in the middle of the
plate and rest the celeriac fondant around and against it. Overlap another piece of turbot
over the celeriac. Spoon the foam over the fish and sprinkle with some sorrel cress.

Scallops and Black Pudding
with sparkling wine sauce and apple rings

Scallops and black pudding are a classic combination and the apple rings set them off a treat.

Serves 4

Sauce
50g butter
2 round shallots, peeled
  and finely chopped
150ml sparkling wine
75ml good fish stock
1 tsp Dijon mustard
100ml double cream
1 handful flat-leaf parsley, chopped

Black pudding
olive oil
12 slices of black pudding

Scallops
12 king scallops, muscle removed
  with roe attached
pinch of dried scallop roe
olive oil

Apple rings and sage leaves
1 Granny Smith apple,
  peeled and cored
squeeze of lemon juice
vegetable oil
knob of butter
1 handful of sage leaves

To prepare the sauce
Melt the butter in a large frying pan, add the shallots and cook until softened. Deglaze the pan with sparkling wine and reduce by half. Strain into a clean pan, then add the fish stock and continue to reduce. Whisk in the mustard, double cream and a small handful of chopped parsley and reduce until you get the desired consistency.

tip:
You don't need the scallop roes for this recipe, but don't throw them away. Poach them for 30 seconds and they are brilliant scattered over a salad or mixed in with a salad dressing.

To cook the black pudding
Warm a touch of olive oil in a non-stick frying pan and cook the black pudding rounds for 1–2 minutes each side until golden. Set aside to keep warm.

To cook the scallops
Sprinkle the scallops with the dried roe, season lightly with salt and pepper and coat with a little olive oil. Heat a griddle pan until smoking hot and sear the scallops on each side for 1–2 minutes until they start to caramelise. Remove and set aside.

To prepare the apple rings and sage leaves

Peel the apples, remove the core and slice into rings. Drizzle with lemon juice. Heat a little oil in a frying pan and fry the apples on each side until golden. Add a knob of butter towards the end and allow to caramelise.

Heat 2–3 tablespoons of vegetable oil in a frying pan and fry the sage leaves for a few seconds on each side until golden. Remove and drain on kitchen paper.

To serve

Arrange three apple rings on each plate. Top each one with a slice of black pudding, followed by a scallop and a sage leaf. Pour over the sauce.

County chef:
Sue Ellis
Restaurant:
Belle House

Head chef at the Belle House in Pershore, Sue Ellis was listed in *The Independent*'s 2008 list of ten female chefs to watch and has won a number of other awards. Sue was born and bred in Worcestershire but left to work in London for a while with chefs such as Gordon Ramsay and Thomas Keller. She is happy to be back in her home county and is very proud of the local produce.

Nearly all her suppliers are local and she keeps in constant touch with them to find out what is on the way. She has had a classical training and sees her food as modern versions of the classics.

"We hit Worcestershire at the end of April, slap bang in the middle of asparagus season. It's a major crop here – Vale of Evesham asparagus has been thought the best in the world for years – so it was asparagus madness all over the county. The best time to eat asparagus, as with most fruit and veg, is when it's growing. So many of the producers we visited around the country extolled the virtues of seasonal eating and the asparagus growers were no exception. Out-of-season produce, flown in from miles away, just isn't the same thing at all. We went out picking the little beauties and rode in an asparagus buggy – asparagus is the only crop you can pick sitting down! It was really good fun and we picked purple asparagus as well as green.

Pears are another speciality of this wonderful county and they also make a drink from them called perry. We met Richard Reynolds who makes perry in his garage and we got quite a taste for the drink. Good for cooking with, too."

Worcestershire

Malvern Pudding

This apple and custard pudding is traditionally served cold, but we liked it bubbling hot. We got this recipe from the museum in Malvern and cooked it the proper way.

Serves 4–6

Apple filling	**Topping**
50g butter	110g butter
1kg cooking apples, peeled and sliced	50g cornflour
	825ml milk
50g granulated sugar	50g granulated sugar
zest of 2 lemons	2 eggs, beaten
	50g demerara sugar
	½ tsp ground cinnamon

To cook the apples

Heat a large saucepan, add the butter and apples and cook for 4–5 minutes until the apples have softened and broken down. Add the sugar and lemon zest and cook for a few more minutes. Pour into a heatproof dish.

To make the topping

Preheat the grill to medium hot. Heat a saucepan and melt half the butter. Stir in the cornflour and cook for another 2 minutes until thickened and smooth. Add the milk, whisking all the time, and cook until thickened – 2–3 minutes.

Remove the pan from the heat and add the granulated sugar and beaten eggs, whisking well. Spoon the topping over the cooked apple in the heatproof dish. Mix the demerara sugar and cinnamon together and sprinkle over the top, then dot with the remaining butter. Place the pudding under the grill until golden brown and bubbling. Serve immediately.

did you know?
Traditional puddings like this are said to be dying out because no one makes them anymore. This is one we think deserves bringing back – it's really good.

Sue Ellis's Pigeon Breast in Pastry

with artichoke purée and purple-sprouting broccoli

This is a great way to serve pigeon and the sweet saltiness of the air-dried ham really goes well with the broccoli.

Serves 4

Pigeons in pastry

4 breasts Peopleton pigeon,
   plucked and with no shot!
25g butter
1 sprig of thyme
1 tbsp local honey
2 sheets of filo pastry
2 egg yolks, whisked
150ml red wine jus made from pigeon bones

Artichoke purée

8 large Pershore Jerusalem artichokes
1 tbsp vitamin C powder

1 large Vale potato, peeled
300ml milk
25g butter

Potatoes

3 large Vale potatoes, peeled
butter
1 tsp cornflour

Broccoli

2 slices air-dried ham, cut into strips
1 head Eckthington purple-sprouting
   broccoli, trimmed into florets

tip:

*See the note on page
68 about the sous-vide
method of cooking.*

To cook the pigeon breasts
Put the pigeon breasts in a sealed vacuum bag with half the butter, thyme, honey and seasoning and cook for 20 minutes at 64°C in a sous-vide water bath. This will allow the breasts to cook through thoroughly, but still have a pinkish hue. Remove the breasts from the bag, allow to cool and pat dry.

Cut the filo pastry into 4cm strips. Brush a strip with egg wash, place another filo strip on top, brush with egg and repeat until you have 4 piles of 4 strips each. Keep the pastry under a damp cloth. Starting from one end of the strip, roll up each pigeon breast in filo pastry to form a parcel. Place them on a baking sheet and brush with remaining egg wash. When you are almost ready to serve, preheat the oven to 180°C/Gas 4. Cook the pigeon parcels for 6 minutes until the pastry is golden. Leave to rest for a few minutes before serving.

To prepare the artichoke purée
Peel the Jerusalem artichokes and slice them finely. As you work, drop the slices into water in which you have dissolved the vitamin C powder – this prevents them going black.

Take a potato about the same size as the artichokes and slice it into the milk in a saucepan. Drain the artichokes and add them to the milk, discarding the vitamin C water. Bring to the boil and simmer until tender, then blend with a hand blender until smooth. Add the remaining butter, season and keep warm.

To cook the broccoli and the potatoes

Place the air-dried ham on a tray under the grill and cook it until crisp. Blanch the purple-sprouting broccoli until tender and season. Peel the potatoes into cylinders, then slice them on a Chinese mandolin. Brush the slices with butter, season and dust with a little cornflour. Place the slices on a baking mat in a flower shape and then build up the layers until the stack is 4 slices deep. Place another mat on top and then cook in the oven for 8–10 minutes until golden and crisp.

To serve

Place a pigeon breast on each plate with a swipe of artichoke purée next to it. Add some purple-sprouting broccoli with the air-dried ham sprinkled over the top. Then add some potatoes and warmed-through red wine jus. Some spinach is a good accompaniment.

County chef:
Andrew Pern
Restaurant:
The Star Inn

A Michelin-starred pub on the
Yorkshire Moors, The Star Inn
is run by Andrew, head chef,
and his wife Jacquie who's in
charge of front of house. They
took over the 14th-century pub
in 1996 when it was in ruins
and have transformed it, restoring the beautiful thatched
building to its former glory.

They enjoy being part of the
community and local suppliers
beat a path to their door with
meat, fish, veg, fruit, herbs
and honey, all of which feature
in the Star's menu, written up
on a blackboard every lunchtime and evening. Andrew
was born in nearby Whitby
and used to visit the Star Inn
when he was a child.

Take a potato about the same size as the artichokes and slice it into the milk in a saucepan. Drain the artichokes and add them to the milk, discarding the vitamin C water. Bring to the boil and simmer until tender, then blend with a hand blender until smooth. Add the remaining butter, season and keep warm.

To cook the broccoli and the potatoes

Place the air-dried ham on a tray under the grill and cook it until crisp. Blanch the purple-sprouting broccoli until tender and season. Peel the potatoes into cylinders, then slice them on a Chinese mandolin. Brush the slices with butter, season and dust with a little cornflour. Place the slices on a baking mat in a flower shape and then build up the layers until the stack is 4 slices deep. Place another mat on top and then cook in the oven for 8–10 minutes until golden and crisp.

To serve

Place a pigeon breast on each plate with a swipe of artichoke purée next to it. Add some purple-sprouting broccoli with the air-dried ham sprinkled over the top. Then add some potatoes and warmed-through red wine jus. Some spinach is a good accompaniment.

County chef:
Andrew Pern
Restaurant:
The Star Inn

A Michelin-starred pub on the Yorkshire Moors, The Star Inn is run by Andrew, head chef, and his wife Jacquie who's in charge of front of house. They took over the 14th-century pub in 1996 when it was in ruins and have transformed it, restoring the beautiful thatched building to its former glory.

They enjoy being part of the community and local suppliers beat a path to their door with meat, fish, veg, fruit, herbs and honey, all of which feature in the Star's menu, written up on a blackboard every lunchtime and evening. Andrew was born in nearby Whitby and used to visit the Star Inn when he was a child.

Take a potato about the same size as the artichokes and slice it into the milk in a saucepan. Drain the artichokes and add them to the milk, discarding the vitamin C water. Bring to the boil and simmer until tender, then blend with a hand blender until smooth. Add the remaining butter, season and keep warm.

To cook the broccoli and the potatoes

Place the air-dried ham on a tray under the grill and cook it until crisp. Blanch the purple-sprouting broccoli until tender and season. Peel the potatoes into cylinders, then slice them on a Chinese mandolin. Brush the slices with butter, season and dust with a little cornflour. Place the slices on a baking mat in a flower shape and then build up the layers until the stack is 4 slices deep. Place another mat on top and then cook in the oven for 8–10 minutes until golden and crisp.

To serve

Place a pigeon breast on each plate with a swipe of artichoke purée next to it. Add some purple-sprouting broccoli with the air-dried ham sprinkled over the top. Then add some potatoes and warmed-through red wine jus. Some spinach is a good accompaniment.

Stuffed Pork Fillet
with pear and perry sauce, fondant sweet potatoes and asparagus

Pears are a Worcestershire speciality and a drink called perry, similar to cider, is made from them. It made a great sauce that went beautifully with this pork.

Serves 4

Pork

800g pork fillet

1 horseshoe of black pudding, skin removed

250g thin streaky bacon or pancetta, stretched thin over the back of a knife

4 sage leaves, cut into strips

Pear and perry sauce

25g butter

1 tbsp muscovado sugar

3 pears, peeled, cored and quartered

1 onion, finely chopped

1 tbsp olive oil

150g button mushrooms, finely sliced

1 bouquet garni (celery, parsley, and bay leaf)

250ml Worcestershire perry

2 tsp Dijon mustard

200ml double cream

2 tbsp roughly chopped flat-leaf parsley,

Fondant sweet potatoes

4 good sweet potatoes, peeled

150g butter

1 garlic clove, lightly crushed

1 sprig of thyme

75ml chicken stock

Asparagus

1kg asparagus

1 tbsp double cream

1 tsp lemon juice

zest of ½ lemon

50g butter

To prepare the pork

Preheat the oven to 180°C/Gas 4. Cut a slash down the pork fillet and form a pocket down its length. Make the black pudding into a sausage shape and use it to stuff the pocket. Place a sheet of clingfilm on to a board and lay the stretched bacon or pancetta slices on top to form a rectangular sheet of meat. Put the stuffed loin on to the bacon, across the end of the rashers. Lay the sage leaf strips on to the top of the pork. Season with the sea salt flakes and freshly ground black pepper and roll up, using the clingfilm to help you make a tidy shape. Carefully roll the meat out of the clingfilm on to an oiled baking sheet with the loose ends of the bacon tucked underneath the roll.

tip:

Take care when cooking sweet potatoes. They contain a lot of sugar so burn easily and you don't want them black!

Heat the oil in a frying pan and place the roll, join-side down, into the hot oil to seal it. Fry until the bacon jacket starts to colour, then place in the oven for about 20 minutes. Remove and leave to rest for at least 10 minutes. Save any meat juices for the sauce.

To make the sauce

Melt the butter in a frying pan, add the sugar and cook for a few minutes to make a caramel. Add the pears and cook for about 10 minutes until tender, turning occasionally to coat in the caramel. Remove from the heat and set aside.

In a separate frying pan, sweat the onion in the olive oil for 3–4 minutes until translucent. Add the mushrooms and cook for another minute or two. Add the bouquet garni, perry and mustard, season with salt and pepper and simmer for 10 minutes until the perry has reduced. Add the cream, parsley, meat juices from the pork and the caramelised pears and warm through, but do not allow to boil.

To make the fondant potatoes

Cut the potatoes into 2cm rounds, then using a cutter, cut out perfect discs. Cut off the sharp corners to make nice barrel shapes. Melt the butter in a pan and add the garlic and thyme. Add the sweet potato rounds and cook until just coloured on the bottom. When the potatoes are starting to colour, turn them over. Add the stock very carefully as it will splutter and explode everywhere! Season well, then simmer for 10–15 minutes until tender.

To prepare the asparagus

to serve:

Slice the pork thickly and lay 3 slices on each plate, with a piece of sweet potato between each slice. Place a spoonful of asparagus purée to one side, then lay the asparagus tips in a fan around it. Spoon the pears and sauce around.

If the asparagus is early season or a bit woody, it is best to peel it. Cut off the tips about 2cm down the stems and set aside. Cut the stalks into 1cm long pieces. Bring a pan of salted water to the boil, add the asparagus stalks and simmer for 3–4 minutes until tender. Keep a close eye on them so they don't get soggy. Put the cooked stalks into a blender, add the cream and process to a fine purée. Add the lemon juice and zest and blitz again. Adjust the seasoning and transfer to a saucepan for reheating later.

Bring another pan of salted water to the boil, add the asparagus tips and blanch for 3 minutes until just cooked. Drain and plunge into iced cold water immediately to stop the cooking process. This keeps the colour perfect and ensures that the tips are not overcooked. Before serving, refresh the tips in a little hot water and butter in a frying pan.

County chef:
Andrew Pern
Restaurant:
The Star Inn

A Michelin-starred pub on the Yorkshire Moors, The Star Inn is run by Andrew, head chef, and his wife Jacquie who's in charge of front of house. They took over the 14th-century pub in 1996 when it was in ruins and have transformed it, restoring the beautiful thatched building to its former glory.

They enjoy being part of the community and local suppliers beat a path to their door with meat, fish, veg, fruit, herbs and honey, all of which feature on the Star's menu, written up on a blackboard every lunchtime and evening. Andrew was born in nearby Whitby and used to visit the Star Inn when he was a child.

" Yorkshire is big and beautiful. It has big skies, big landscapes – and people like big portions of good food. Yorkshire people love their county and they're proud of it, with good reason. We know Yorkshire well and, since it was Si's birthday while we were there, we didn't hesitate to revisit the Magpie Café in Whitby for the best fish and chips ever. What a place. If you don't know it, go there – soon. When we'd finished scoffing, we found that there are some enterprising producers in the county. A great example is Andrew Henshaw who runs Mainsgill Farm, near Richmond, with his wife Marie. This has grown into quite an empire – they rear their own livestock and cure meat on the premises, as well as running a farm shop, butchers' shop and café. You really can get most of your weekly shop from them. Andrew and Marie saw an opportunity and took it, and they deserve their success as their produce is great. And they have a camel out the back. We cooked their Black Porky sausages with our Yorkshire pud – which is of course, the best – in our mobile kitchen and a great time was had by all. "

North Yorkshire

Yorkshire Pudding and Black Porkies
with beer and onion gravy

Everyone thinks we make the best Yorkshire pud and it's true – we do. We use Dave's mam's recipe and he has her foolproof Yorkshire pudding tin that dates back to World War II. Ask your butcher for marrow bones for the stock. They can be rib, short rib, knuckle, thigh, for example, and should have a bit of meat on them. Ask for the beef fat too.

Serves 4

Beef stock (makes 1.5 litres)
1kg marrow bones

2 large onions, cut into quarters

2 carrots, peeled and cut into quarters

2 celery sticks, cut in half

350ml bottle of local North Yorkshire light beer

1 bouquet garni (parsley, bay leaves, thyme)

4 garlic cloves, unpeeled

10 black peppercorns

1 tsp tomato paste

1.5 litres water

12 Black Porkies (or similar black pudding sausages)

Gravy
50g beef fat

2 onions, finely chopped

1.5 litres beef stock

175ml Yorkshire beer

1 tbsp redcurrant jelly

Yorkshire pudding
4 heaped tbsp of plain flour

½ tsp salt

2 eggs, beaten

275ml full fat milk

2–3 tbsp vegetable oil, such as sunflower, or a blob of goose fat

tip:

If your gravy isn't as thick as you'd like, make a smooth, wet paste with 2 tsp of flour and 2 tsp of water. Slowly add this to the gravy, stirring all the time, and cook for another couple of minutes to cook out the flour, before adding the redcurrant jelly. Any left-over stock can be frozen in ice cube trays and kept for up to 6 months in the freezer.

To make the stock
Preheat the oven to 230°C/Gas 8. Put the bones in a roasting pan, sprinkle with salt flakes and roast for 30 minutes or until well browned. Add the onions, carrots and celery and return to the oven until the vegetables are also browned.

Tip everything into a stockpot. Put the roasting tin on top of the stove, pour in half the beer and deglaze the roasting tin to release all those lovely caramelised meaty juices. Bring the beer and juices to the boil, then pour the beery liquid into the stockpot – you'll start to smell how great this stock is going to be!

Add the bouquet garni, garlic, peppercorns and tomato paste to the stockpot. Pour in the water and bring slowly to the boil. Skim the fat off the stock and simmer gently for 2 hours. Strain, leave to cool and skim any remaining fat before using.

To make the gravy

Slice the beef fat into thin strips – you'll need about 10. Put the fat in a large frying pan, sprinkle with salt and fry for a couple of minutes until it begins to melt. Remove any unmelted strips and discard. Add the onions to the pan and sauté until soft and translucent. Pour in half the beef stock and beer, bring to the boil and simmer for at least 15 minutes. The longer you simmer it, the thicker the gravy will be so it's up to you. Add the redcurrant jelly about 5 minutes before you finish simmering the gravy and stir it in. Season and serve.

To make the Yorkshire puddings

Preheat the oven to 220°C/Gas 7. Sieve the flour with the salt into a bowl and make a well in the centre. Gradually work in the beaten eggs, then whisk in the milk – the consistency should be like single cream. Leave the batter to stand for at least an hour. You'll need some Yorkshire pudding tins, either individual ones or one big tin.

to serve:
Serve some Yorkshire pudding on to each plate and add the sausages. Pour over the gravy and enjoy!

Put the oil or goose fat into your Yorkshire pudding tin and put it in the oven for at least 5 minutes, until it's smoking hot. Give the batter a stir, pour it into the tin and watch it sizzle! Quickly put the tin into the oven and bake for about 30 minutes or until the pudding has risen to golden-brown perfection – for individual puds, cook for 10–15 minutes. Meanwhile cook the sausages in a frying pan over a medium heat for 20–25 minutes.

Andrew Pern's Harome-reared duck
with garden thyme mash and Yorkshire sauce

Andrew's deconstructed duck is a great way of dealing with this bird, as the various parts benefit from different cooking methods. The legs are best slow-cooked while the breast should be left pink or you miss out on its flavour. This way you get the best of both.

Serves 4

Duck
4 duck legs
1 litre duck fat
1 star anise
1 bay leaf
4 duck chipolatas
2 duck breasts

Sauce
1 orange
200ml red wine
150g caster sugar

110g redcurrant jelly
110ml duck jus

Potato, eggs and duck liver
500g mashed potato
110g butter
110ml whipping cream
10g lemon thyme, leaves picked off the stems
4 duck eggs
white wine vinegar
1 tbsp olive oil
300g duck liver

To prepare the duck
Preheat the oven to 140°C/Gas 1. Put the duck legs into a roasting tin or ovenproof frying pan, add the duck fat, star anise and bay leaf and cook in the oven for 2½ hours. Remove and once the duck legs have cooled down, split the thigh and the drumstick and put them on a baking tray.

Turn up the oven to 190°C/Gas 5. Grill the chipolatas until just cooked and put them on the baking tray with the legs and thighs. Pan-fry the duck breasts until the skin is crispy but still there. Add them to the baking tray and put everything in the preheated oven for 5 minutes.

To make the Yorkshire sauce
Peel the orange and cut the peel into julienne strips, removing all the white pith. Place the strips in a pan with the red wine, sugar and redcurrant jelly. Juice the orange and pour that into the pan as well. Reduce until the liquid becomes syrup and add the duck jus.

To prepare the potatoes, eggs and duck liver

Boil the potatoes, drain and mash. Put the butter and cream into a saucepan, bring to the boil and cook until reduced by half. Add this to the mash and mix well to make a smooth purée. Season with salt and pepper, then add the lemon thyme leaves and mix well. Spoon into a piping bag and keep warm.

Poach the duck eggs in simmering water with a little white wine vinegar for about 3 minutes and keep warm. Heat a frying pan until hot, add a little oil, then the duck liver and fry on each side for 1–2 minutes until it becomes spongy.

tip:

When the duck legs are done the meat starts to shrink back from the bone and you'll see little white flecks in the bone – this shows that the leg is cooked properly.

To serve

Pipe five turrets of mash around the outside of the plate and one in the centre. On one turret of mash, place a piece of duck drumstick, then add a piece of thigh, a chipolata, liver and poached egg to the other turrets. Cut the duck breast into slices and place a few on the turret in the centre of the plate. Drizzle the Yorkshire sauce around and over the dish and serve immediately.

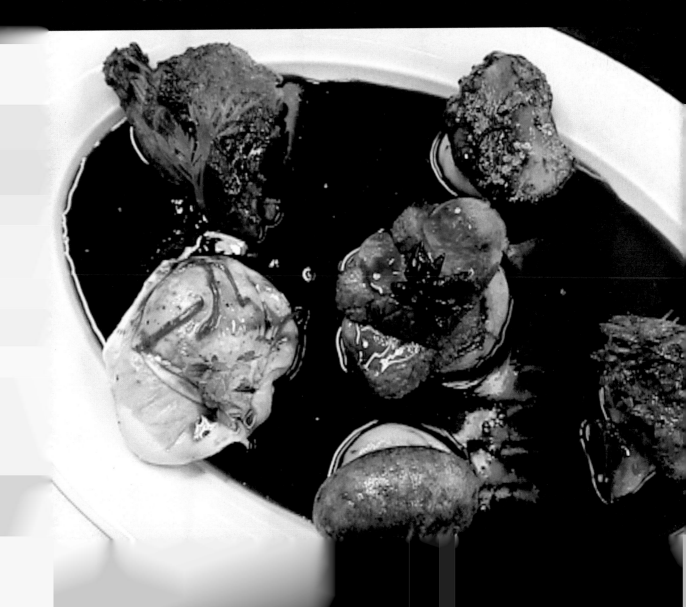

Turbot
with langoustines and sandefjord sauce

Turbot is such a great fish and needs very little doing to it. Simple
is best with some tasty accompaniments such as this creamy sauce.
The langoustines add a touch of luxury.

Serves 4

110g butter
2 turbot, filleted
16 langoustines
16 new potatoes, barrel cut
12 baby leeks
butter

Sauce
200ml single cream
2 star anise
200g unsalted butter, diced
1–2 tbsp finely chopped chives
1–2 tbsp finely chopped dill
zest of ½ lemon

To prepare the turbot and langoustines
Heat a frying pan, add the butter and turbot fillets and cook them on each side for
2–3 minutes until just cooked. Bring a large pan of salted water to the boil, add the
langoustines and boil for 3–4 minutes, then drain. Set 4 whole ones aside as a garnish.

To make it easier to get the meat out of the rest of the langoustines, part of the shell needs
to be removed. Turn the langoustines over to reveal the belly and using a pair of scissors,
cut along each side and remove the shell to expose the sweet and tender meat.

To cook the potatoes and leeks
Put the potatoes into a pan of water, bring to the boil and simmer until done. Drain and
toss in a little butter, salt and black pepper. Bring a separate pan of water to the boil, add
the leeks and cook for 3–4 minutes until tender. Drain, toss with a little butter, salt and
black pepper.

To make the sauce
Pour the cream into a saucepan, add the star anise and bring to the boil, then simmer
until reduced by half. Gradually beat in the butter, a little at a time. When all the butter
is incorporated, remove the pan from the heat. Add the chives, dill and lemon zest and
season with salt and black pepper to taste.

To serve
Place a turbot fillet on the centre of each plate. Add the shelled langoustines, potatoes
and leeks, then spoon over the sauce. Garnish each plate with a whole langoustine.

Suppliers

Here are the details for farms, growers, shops and other suppliers we visited on our travels, and the great restaurants where we held our cook-offs.

Aberdeenshire

The Store (Aberdeen Angus beef)
Foveran, Newburgh, Ellon AB41 6AY
01358 788083

The Oats of Alford (oats)
Montgarrie Mill, , Alford AB33 8AP
01561 377356
www.oatmealofalford.com

Restaurant: **The Milton**
Crathes, Banchory AB31 5QH
01330 844 566
www.themilton.co.uk

Anglesey

Hooton's Homegrown (Farm shop)
Gwydryn Hir, Brynsiencyn LL61 6HQ
01248 430344
www.hootonshomegrown.com

Menai Oysters (mussels and oysters)
Tal-y-Bont Bach, Llanfairpwll LL61 6UU
01248 430878
www.menaioysters.co.uk

Halen Mon Sea Salt (sea salt)
The Anglesey Sea Salt Company Ltd,
Brynsiencyn LL61 6TQ
01248 430871
www.seasalt.co.uk

Restaurant: **Noelle's**
Tre-Ysgawen Hall, Llangefni LL77 7UR
0871 223 9401
www.treysgawen-hall.co.uk

Antrim

RJ Cherry & Son (potatoes)
38-40 Carnlea Road, Ballymena BT43 6TS
028 2568 5535
www.rjcherryandson.com

Atlantic Ocean Delights
(dulse seaweed)
Robert McColm, 51 Quinton Avenue
Magheramorne, Larne BT40 3JH
07523 620290
amccolm@519hotmail.com

Restaurant: **James Street South**
21 James Street South,
Belfast BT2 7GA
028 9043 4310
www.jamesstreetsouth.co.uk

Argyll & Bute

Springbank Distillery (whisky)
85 Longrow, Campbeltown PA28 6EX
01586 552009
www.springbankwhisky.com

Restaurant: **Kilberry Inn**
Kilberry PA29 6YD
01880 770223
www.kilberryinn.com

Carmarthenshire

Parson's Pickles (cockles and laver)
Leslie A. Parsons & Sons
(Burry Port) Ltd, Ashburnham Works,
Burry Port SA16 0ET
01554 833351
www.parsonspickles.co.uk

Fferm Tyllwyd (Welsh black cattle)
Fferm Tyllwyd, Felingwm,
Uchaf SA32 7QE
01267 290537
www.organicwelshblackbeef.co.uk

Cothi Valley Goats
(goat's cheese & meat)
Cilwr Farm, Talley, Llandeilo SA19 7BQ
01558 685555
www.goats-cheese-online.co.uk

Restaurant: **Y Polyn**
Capel Dewi, Nantgaredig SA32 7LH
01267 290000
www.ypolynrestaurant.co.uk

Cheshire

Joseph Heler Cheese
(Cheshire cheese)
Laurels Farm, Nantwich CW5 7PE
01270 841500
www.joseph-heler.co.uk

Holly Tree Farm (Hogget)
Chester Road, Over Tabley,
Nr Knutsford
01565 651835
www.hollytreefarmshop.co.uk

Cheshire Smokehouse
(Smoked products)
Vost Farm, Morely Green,
Wilmslow SK9 5NU
01625 548499
www.cheshiresmokehouse.co.uk

Restaurant: **Belle Epoque**
60 King Street, Knutsford WA16 6DT
01565 632661
www.thebelleepoque.com

Cornwall

Fish For Thought
(fish and shellfish)
Unit 1A, Victoria Business Park,
Roche, St Austell PL26 8LX
01726 891556
www.fishforthought.co.uk

Tregothnan (tea)
The Woodyard, Tregothnan,
Truro TR2 4AJ
01872 520325
www.tregothnan.co.uk

Restaurant: **Viners**
Carvynick, Summercourt,
Newquay TR8 5AF
01872 510 544
www.vinersrestaurant.co.uk

Derbyshire

Calke Abbey *(Venison)*
The Calke Estate, Calke Abbey
Ticknall, Derby DE73 7LE
01332 863822

Restaurant: **Fischer's Baslow Hall**
Calver Road, Baslow, Derbyshire,DE45 1RR
01246 583259
www.fischers-baslowhall.co.uk

Dumfries & Galloway

Stuart Houston Butchers *(haggis)*
JB Houston, Greenbrae Loaning DG1 3DQ
01387 255528
www.jbhouston.co.uk

Weatherall Food *(mutton)*
Weatherall Foods Limited,
Crochmore House, Irongray DG2 9SF
01387 730326

John Mellis's Honey *(honey)*
Cleuch House, Auldgirth DG2 0TP
01848 331280

Restaurant: **Auchen Castle**
Beattock, Near Moffat DG10 9SH
01683 300407
www.auchencastle.com

Essex

Colchester Oyster Fishery *(oysters)*
Pyefleet Quay, Mersea Island
Colchester CO5 8UN
01206 384141
www.colchesteroysterfishery.com

Kelly Turkey Farms *(turkeys)*
Springate Farm, Bicknacre Road
Danbury CM3 4EP
01245 223581
www.kelly-turkeys.com

Tiptree Conserves *(jams and jellies)*
Wilkin & Sons Limited, Tiptree CO5 0RF
01621 815407
www.tiptree.com

Restaurant: **Baumann's Brasserie**
4-6 Stoneham Street, Coggeshall CO6 1TT
01376 561453
www.baumannsbrasserie.co.uk

Fermanagh

O'Doherty's Fine Meats
(black bacon and other meats)
Belmore Street, Enniskillen BT74 6AA
028 6632 2152
www.blackbacon.com

Orchard Acre Farm *(herbs)*
Moynaghan North Road,
Lisnarick, Irvinestown BT94 1LQ
028 686 21066
www.orchardacrefarm.com

Restaurant: **Lough Erne Golf Resort**
Belleek Road, Enniskillen BT93 7ED
028 6632 3230
www.loughernegolfresort.com

Gloucestershire

Great Farm *(guinea fowl)*
Great Farm, Whelford, Fairford GL7 4EA
01285 712316

R-Oil *(rapeseed oil)*
Swell Buildings Farm, Lower Swell,
Stow on the Wold GL54 1HG
01451 870387
www.r-oil.co.uk

Restaurant: **Allium**
1 London Street, Market Place,
Fairford GL7 4AH
01285 712200
www.allium.uk.net

Gwynedd

Aberdovey Butchers *(lamb)*
3 Copperhill Street, Aberdovey LL35 0EU
01654 767267

Cynan Jones *(mushrooms)*
Glan Meirion, Bedd Gelert LL55 4YG
01766 890353

Restaurant: **Maes Y Neuadd**
Talsarnau LL47 6YA
01766 780200
www.neuadd.com

Hampshire

Laverstoke Park Farm
(wild boar and pork)
Overton RG25 3DR
01256 772813
www.laverstokepark.co.uk

Mrs Tee's Wild Mushrooms
(mushrooms)
Gorsemeadow, Sway Road,
Lymington SO41 8LR
01590 673354
www.wildmushrooms.co.uk

Restaurant: **Le Poussin**
Parkhill, Beaulieu Road,
Lyndhurst SO43 7FZ
02380 282944
www.lepoussin.co.uk

Herefordshire

Free Town Herefords *(beef)*
Tarrington, Hereford HR1 4JB
01432 890238
www.free-town.co.uk/farm/farminfo.html

L'Escargot Anglais *(snails)*
Credenhill Snail Farm, Credenhill,
Hereford HR4 7DN
01432 760218

Jo Hilditch *(cassis)*
Jo Hilditch British Cassis,
Whittern Farms Ltd,
Lyonshall HR5 3JA
01544 340241
www.britishcassis.co.uk

Restaurant: **The Bridge at Wilton**
Ross on Wye HR9 6AA
01989 562655
www.bridge-house-hotel.com

Kent

Brogdale Farm (cobnuts)
Brogdale Road, Faversham ME13 8XZ
01795 536250
www.brogdalecollections.co.uk

Fergus Drennan (seaweeds)
Forager
fergustheforager@lycos.com
http://www.wildmanwildfood.com

Shepherd Neame Brewery (beer)
17 Court Street, Faversham ME13 7AX
01795 532206
www.shepherd-neame.co.uk

Restaurant: **Read's**
Macknade Manor, Canterbury Road,
Faversham ME13 8XE
01795 535344
www.reads.com

Lancashire

Johnson & Swarbrick
(Goosnargh ducks)
Swainson House Farm, Goosnargh,
Preston PR3 2JU
01772 865 251
http://myweb.tiscali.co.uk/
jandsgoosnargh/default.htm

Nelson's Farm
(Ormskirk new potatoes)
Mossville, Moss Lane,
Burscough L40 4BA
01704 892 599

Restaurant: **Northcote**
Northcote Road, Blackburn BB6 8BE
01254 240555
www.northcote.com

Leicestershire

Blackbrook Longhorns
(Leicestershire Longhorn beef)
Springbarrow Lodge, Swannymote Road
Grace Dieu, Nr Coalville LE67 5UT
01509 503276
www.blackbrook-longhorns.com

Tuxford & Tebbutt (Stilton)
The Cheese Company Ltd, Thorpe End,
Melton Mowbray LE13 1RB
01664 502903
www.tuxfordandtebbutt.co.uk

Restaurant: **The Red Lion Inn**
Red Lion Street, Stathern LE14 4HS
01949 860 868
www.theredlioninn.co.uk

Lincolnshire

Woodlands Farm
(Lincoln Red beef and
Lincoln Longwool lamb)
Kirton House, Kirton, Boston PE20 1JD
01205 724778
www.woodlandsfarm.co.uk

Windy Ridge Veg
(cauliflower and other veg)
Hubberts Bridge Rd, Kirton Holme,
Boston PE20 1TW
01205 290274

Restaurant: **Winteringham Fields**
1 Silver Street,
Winteringham DN15 9ND
01724 733096
www.winteringhamfields.com

Monmouthshire

Trealy Farm Charcuterie
(Charcuterie Products)
Mitchel Troy NP25 4BL
01600 740705
www.trealyfarm.com

Parva Farm Vineyard
(mead and wine)
Trelleck Road, Tintern Parva,
Chepstow NP16 6SQ
01291 689636
www.mim.adventa.org.uk

Restaurant: **The Hardwick**
Old Raglan Road,
Abergavenny NP7 9AA
01873 854220
www.thehardwick.co.uk

Morayshire

Lossie Seafoods Ltd
(smoked salmon)
2 March Road Industrial Estate,
Buckie AB56 4BY
01542 831000
www.lossieseafoods.com

Ballindalloch Estate Wild Salmon
(wild salmon)
Ballindalloch Castle,
Ballindalloch AB37 9AX
01807 500 205
www.ballindallochcastle.co.uk

Restaurant: **Mansefield Hotel**
Mayne Road, The Royal Burgh of Elgin
01343 540883
www.themansefield.com

Norfolk

Great Snoring Quail/ E J Perowne
(eggs)
Top Farm, Great Snoring,
Fakenham NR21 0HW
01328 820351

R W & J A Davies Fishmongers
(Cromer crabs)
7 Garden St, Cromer NR27 9HN
01263 514517

Restaurant: **Morston Hall**
Morston, Holt NR25 7AA
01263 741041
www.morstonhall.com

Oxfordshire

Foxbury Farm (farm shop and butcher)
Burford Road, Brize Norton OX18 3NX
01993 844141
www.foxburyfarm.co.uk

**Alex James' Cheeses –
Evenlode Enterprises**
(goat's cheese)
P.O Box 256, Chipping Norton OX7 9BX
01608 658929
www.evenlodepartnership.co.uk

Quince Products
01491 614 664
www.quinceproducts.co.uk

Restaurant: **Kingham Plough**
Kingham,
Chipping Norton OX7 6YD
01608 658327
www.thekinghamplough.co.uk

Shropshire

Ludlow Food Centre
(gammon and other produce)
Bromfield, Ludlow SY8 2JR
01584 856000
www.ludlowfoodcentre.co.uk

The Ludlow Jam Pan
(preserves)
The Gardener's Cottage,
12 Overton,,Nr. Ludlow SY8 4DY
01584 872 965

Restaurant: **La Bécasse**
17 Corve Street, Ludlow SY8 1DA
01584 872 325
www.labecasse.co.uk

Somerset

West Croft Cider Farm (cider)
Brent Knoll, Highbridge TA9 4BE
Tel: 01278 760762

West Country Water Buffalo
(buffalo)
Lower Oakley Farm,
Chilthorne Domer,
Yeovil BA22 8RQ
01935 840567
www.westcountrywaterbuffalo.com

John Rowswell Baker's Farm
(vegetables)
Barrington, Nr Ilminster TA12 0JB
01460 55504

Restaurant: **The Castle**
Castle Green, Taunton TA1 1NF
01823 272671
www.the-castle-hotel.com

Staffordshire

Essington Fruit Farm *(farm shop)*
Bognop Road, Essington,
Wolverhampton WV112AZ
01902 735724
www.essingtonfarm.co.uk

Packington Poultry *(chicken)*
Blakenhall Park,
Barton-under-Needwood, DE13 8AJ
01283 711547
www.packingtonpoultry.co.uk

Restaurant: **The Moat House**
Lower Penkridge Road,
Acton Trussell ST17 0RJ
01785 712217
www.moathouse.co.uk

Suffolk

Blythburgh Free Range Pork
St Margarets Farm, Mells,
Halesworth IP19 9DD
01986 873298
www.freerangepork.co.uk

The Wild Meat Company *(rabbit)*
Lime Tree Farm, Blaxhall,
Woodbridge IP12 2DY
01728 663 211
www.wildmeat.co.uk

Pakenham Water Mill *(wholemeal flour)*
Mill Road, Pakenham
Bury St Edmunds IP31 2ND
01284 724075
www.pakenhamwatermill.co.uk

Restaurant: **The Bildeston Crown**
High Street, Bildeston IP7 7EB
01449 740510
www.thebildestoncrown.co.uk

East Sussex

Food Fore Thought *(salt marsh lamb)*
Wickham Manor Farm, Pannel Lane
Winchelsea TN36 4AG
01580 830500
www.foodforethought.com

Ridgeview Vineyard
(sparkling wine)
Fragbarrow Lane,
Ditchling Common BN6 8TP
01444 241441
www.ridgeview.co.uk

Restaurant: **Moonrakers**
High Street, Alfriston BN26 5TD
01323 871199
www.moonrakersrestaurant.co.uk

Worcestershire

GW Revill & Son Farm
(asparagus)
Revills Farm Shop
Bourne Road
Defford WR8 9BS
01386 750466

Barbourne Perry *(perry)*
19 York Place
Worcester WR1 3DR
www.barbournecider.co.uk

Restaurant: **Belle House**
Bridge Street
Pershore WR10 2AJ
01386 555055
www.belle-house.co.uk

North Yorkshire

Mainsgill Farm Shop & Tea Room
(veg, meat and other produce)
East Layton
Richmond DL11 7PN
01325 718860
www.mainsgillfarm.co.uk

The Whitby Catch *(fish)*
1 Pier Road
Whitby YO21 3PT
01947 601313
www.thewhitbycatch.co.uk

Restaurant: **The Star Inn**
Harome
Nr Helmsley YO62 5JE
01439 770397
www.thestaratharome.co.uk

Index

Acknowledgments

Huge thanks are due to the following:

We must start with Amanda and Simon Ross at Cactus Television for making the programme possible. It was a huge undertaking and we thank Cactus for making it happen. Thanks also to our commissioner Liam Keelan and to Carla-Maria Lawson and Gerry Melling, at the BBC, for overseeing the project and giving us the airtime to make a project of this scale work. Thanks to Dave Skinner for his idea in the first place, and to Anna Ratcliffe for all her help and hard work.

We owe a big debt of gratitude to our great contributors, the farmers and food producers who appeared in this programme. They filled our bellies and our programmes with foodie delights. They are National Treasures.

As are our great chefs – from one end of the country to the other we cooked with, laughed with and learned from some of the best chefs in the world. Thanks for your inspiration.

The book wouldn't have been possible without the fantastic people at Orion. A great team, who managed to bring a great book together in the short time we had. Thanks to Amanda Harris, Lucie Stericker, Kate Barr and Jinny Johnson, and to Cristian Barnett who took the majority of the food photographs.

We would also like to thank our great crew. Huge thanks and respect to our producer Dave Mynard and directors Duncan Barnes and Stuart Bateup. Thanks, too, to our lovely production manager Lorna (Fozzie) Fossick, associate producers John Bonny and Eleanor Taylor, and to Lucy Sherwood and Sophie Wells. We thank our buddies at Video Heads – Dave Symmons, Mark (Gusto) Goodhew, Siggi Rosen-Rawlings and Rory McKellar. Thanks to Neil Whiteman and Rick Hussey for all your graft.

Huge thanks to home economists Janet Brinkworth, Sammy Jo Squire and Lisa Harrison.

Back at Cactus we'd like to thank Liz Robinson our edit producer, for unravelling the vast amount of footage. Thanks also to our editing team – Rodney Sims, Steve Chan, Joe Haughey, Tracy Joss and Quinton Smith.

Thanks to Anya Noakes and our agents at United Agents, Maureen Vincent and Charles Walker.

Si and Dave